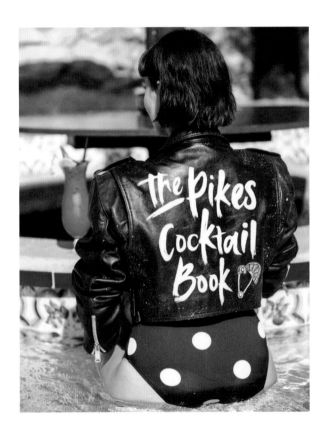

The Pikes Cocktail Book

**ROCK N ROLL
RECIPES FROM THE ICONIC
IBIZAN HOTEL**

RYLAND PETERS & SMALL
LONDON • NEW YORK

CONTENTS

WELCOME
TO PIKES

God, I want a beer. Is that a weird opening to a cocktail book? Maybe, but it's fucking hot and I really want a cold lager in a frosty glass. I've just landed in Ibiza and the first thing that hits you when you leave the airport is the heat. It slaps you right in the face. Sounds obvious, but it's true - the heat, the sun, the noise and the excitement. There's an energy crackling - people dance their way to their taxi and bus pick ups, weaving among the honking taxi drivers. Cares are left at passport control. People come to Ibiza to have fun. And that's exactly what they're going to do. For me, I'm going to think about having that frosty beer.

Hailing a cab from the rank, I thank the gods of air con as I settle into the leather seat and tune into into the generic house beats coming from the stereo. As we head out of the airport under a flawless blue sky, and follow the signs to San Antonio, things couldn't get much more Balearic.

I pay no heed to the vast billboards advertising megastar DJs in San Antonio as they flash by. I'm going somewhere special, I'm heading up into the hills. I'm following in the footsteps of George Michael as he wound his way through the back roads with Andrew Ridgeley to the place where drinks are free; where strangers take you by the hand, and welcome you to wonderland. Fun and sunshine, there's enough for everyone. I'm headed to the original Club Tropicana.

I'm heading to Pikes. Pikes is an iconic Ibizan institution, steeped in rock 'n' roll history and brimming with personality – its famous aquamarine pool was the actual location for a young, tanned and toned George Michael and the infamous Club Tropicana video. And all of it was created by one man, the great, late Tony Pike, who passed away at the age of 86 in early 2019 after leading one of the fullest lives there could be.

The story of how Tony stumbled upon and then decided to create Pikes with his bare hands is Ibizan folklore. But it's all true.

500 years after this fine finca you're standing in was built, Australian yachtsman, businessman and bon viveur Tony Pike washed up on the shores of Ibiza, after being shipwrecked in the Caribbean, hurtling down the Cresta Run and selling superyachts to the rich and famous in Monaco. Tony was persuaded to visit Ibiza by a friend and when he stepped off the ferry he felt a connection with the place. He felt like he was home... When he saw this falling-down farmhouse was called Casa Tonitini, he bought the place.

Tony had a vision – he wanted to build his own hotel and fill it with fun. Over the next 30 years, with the help of his partner Lyn, son Bradley, local builder Phil the Chin and a mob of drunks picked from the Ibizan beaches, he fulfilled this vision. Starting with just a rundown place, a bucket for a toilet and a fire on the kitchen floor, he set to work. The first thing he did was put that famous orange bathroom in Room 1 and things snowballed from there. He stole picture frames from abandoned churches, salvaged double doors from Spanish brothels and, with no real blueprints, architecture know-how or much building experience, built the rooms as and how he saw fit.

People are drawn to the hotel because it's where George Michael sang about the place where "membership's a smiling face", where legends like Grace Jones, Spandau Ballet, Kylie Minogue, Bon Jovi, Tony Curtis, Artwork, Jamie xx, Mark Ronson, Honey Dijon, Robyn, The Black Madonna, Fatboy Slim, DJ Harvey, Naomi Campbell, Julio Iglesias, Ed Sheeran, Arctic Monkeys, Yes, The Vaccines, Disclosure, Sam Smith, Nile Rodgers, LCD Soundsystem, Seth Troxler, Carl Cox, Frank Zappa and many more have partied all night long. Freddie Mercury, of course, loved it here and his 41st birthday was the most lavish party ever seen on the island. Freddie's first performance of Barcelona was in the Potting Shed on back terrace. People come here because they want to have a good time – and nowadays they do it in Freddie Mercury's old bedroom that's been converted into a nightclub.

In 2011, Dawn Hindle and Andy McKay, founders of Ibiza icons Manumission and Ibiza Rocks, took over the hotel, and ensured Tony's vision would carry on. They added more rock 'n' roll with the bands who come to Ibiza to play for them staying, and partying hard, here; the weekend parties; DJ residencies, Sunny's bathroom karaoke and boudoir. They also brought in the amazing Room 39 restaurant with the very highest quality modern cuisine. And, most recently, The Curiosity Shoppe, serving some of the most exciting cocktails on the island - the whole reason you're reading this book.

Tony curated something amazing. The hotel literally has his DNA in it... The walls around the pool will forever ring with Tony's incredible stories - a few of which are recounted in this very book.

Back in the cab, and the driver just skims into the suburbs of the party town of San Antonio but, instead of taking me deeper to the strip, he hangs a right at the roundabout and we head out of town. As you drive away from San Antonio, the roads grow a little quieter, the air seems a bit fresher and the energy relaxes slightly. Local farmers sit and ponder the world outside a taverna with a beer and all the time in the world. Just past this taverna you'll come to a sharp right turn and a battered old sign bearing the name of the hotel. As you drive up the bumpy, lumpy road, you're surrounded by flat, cropless fields and those not in the know might start wondering where a hotel can be. Where are the hoardings, the advertising, the big flashing sign saying, Step this way? There are none. The road goes on just long enough to feel like you've probably, almost definitely, taken a wrong turn, when the car park appears on the right, annotated by a vintage tiled Pikes logo.

I'm here, I must be here. We pull in and park next to the modest entrance, an unassuming portal of just a few steps and a path under an archway that leads between some trees, grass and past what looks like a fake sheep. The air is thick with the scent of lavender and jasmine. I can hear a hubbub from within. A gentle whump whump of some laid-back dub beats. The wind rustles the leaves in the trees and the background vocals of cicadas chirrup endlessly. For just a brief moment, before I walk up those steps, the calm atmosphere belies the extraordinary goings on that occur beyond these walls.

I get out of the taxi, pay the driver, bid him *adios* and, as I turn to close the door, notice, written in huge cursive script, "You can check in, but you can never check out" splashed across the white wall of a barn. This is not the first time I've visited the hotel and seeing this mural always makes me pause. In fact, it becomes stronger each time you return to the hotel. Because it's undeniably true. It's something that everyone who's worked, visited and performed at the hotel knows. There's something about Pikes that you can't quite put your finger on. A feeling, a ball of energy that's within you. You can leave, but it'll stay with you, wherever in the world you head off to. The feeling is the magnet that's been pulling people to the hotel for over 30 years. The DJ Junior Sanchez sums it up, "Pikes is such a magical, mysterious place. The history that it has, has sunken deep into the walls and into the wood of that environment, you can feel the presence of creativity and greatness throughout the hotel..."

This is going to be a fun ride. I take a deep breath, sling my bag over my shoulder and head into the hotel... Cocktail book or not, I'm going to get that ice-cold beer.

I'm fully aware that a stay at Pikes is a marathon and I plan to follow Irvine Welsh's favoured tactic for enjoying the hotel: "It varies on the time of the day," he says, "but in the lazy afternoons I like to grab a lounger by the pool with a cocktail, while in the evening I'll gravitate towards the bar or head upstairs to the restaurant where you have that nice elevated sensation, looking down on the fun but enjoying my nice company, food and wine." Seems reasonable.

The 26-room haven in the San Antonio hills features bespoke rooms and suites set around the sprawling fairytale gardens, the first of which are to my left, shutters drawn, hiding hangovers no doubt. Fake sheep graze in the shade of an ancient tree, a large garden gnome flips me the bird from a bush while what can only be described as vintage American curios are scattered around. The path bears right and I duck through a small glass door into a dark, cool room that a bright pink neon sign announces is the Pikes reception.

The tall, elegant man behind the desk in the thankfully air-conditioned reception is Diego Freta, who has been welcoming guests here for eight years. He smiles warmly, greets me in both Spanish and English and sets about finding my booking. "You'll be in room number 12," he says with a twinkle in his eye. "Is that a good room?" I respond. I can never remember which room is which. Not least because since Tony Pike built them some of the rooms have changed numbers over the years, as the place expanded. "*Si, si* – it's right in the middle of everything, laughs Diego. "Come, I'll take you there." So we leave the pleasant air-conditioned room together and venture back out into the dazzling brightness of the Ibizan sunlight.

There is a breeze though, the eucalyptus tree ahead of me is constantly rustling and fidgeting as the air moves through it and takes the edge off the heat. I hoist my backpack and we wander off into Neverland. We walk past some more sheep grazing in the grass. I'd think they were real but for their neon blue wool. Three cats lounge in the sun, the baked ground warming their lazy bones past yowling into the sunshine. Diego and I walk up a flight of terracotta stairs that bear a cryptic message to all visitors, a line on each step, as you walk up them:

If you are a pretender
Come in!
"Or you wouldn't have come here"
of the dreams
and we are the dream makers
"We're all made here
I'm mad you're mad"
If you are a dreamer
Come sit by my fire

I climb these steps with a furrowed brow (after reading what I realise is a bastardised version of Shel Silverstein's poem) and alight on a large terrace. Suddenly the Ibizan sun feels very hot indeed on the back of my neck as I stand still to take in the view before me. It's right here that Pikes hotel finally reveals itself. It's standing here in this spot that Paul Oakenfold described when he said, "I think there's always a special moment when you walk up those little stairs onto the veranda and you first see the swimming pool with the bar to the left and rooms to the right – that's the Pikes moment, where you're like, 'I'm back!'"

It's true – whether it's your first time or your 100th, there's an overwhelming feeling of familiarity when taking in the scene. It's like the hotel's giving you a warm embrace as you nuzzle into its bosom. It's a view like no other in Ibiza – or anywhere else for that matter. To the right, through some bushes, the terrace overlooks a neon pink and deep green tennis court with a giant disco roller boot parked in one corner. It's a tennis court that has played host to rock concerts, film premieres, screenings, yoga and Goa-influenced cosmic bazaars but precious little, if any, tennis.

A valley of round sofa beds and sun loungers support prone holiday makers in various states of undress. Lounging is the order of the day. As is drinking cocktails. Every guest has a chilled goblet of gin and tonic, Pina Colada, frosty beer or similar to take the edge of off the blistering heat. "I really need one of those drinks," I say to Diego and he laughs as he leads me past the sun worshippers, past the pool and outdoor DJ booth, tantalisingly close to the bar and up some steps into a courtyard.

The original finca is ahead of me, housing the kitchen and legendary nightclub Freddie's with its heavy wooden doors ajar. An enormous bougainvillea rains down from a balcony above me and this courtyard, according to the traditional sign on the wall, is called Plaza Mayor. The courtyard is covered with white awnings gently flapping in the breeze while disco balls of different size and shapes throw sparkling shapes dancing around the walls. To the right are some steps up to a deep blue open-windowed restaurant and cocktail bar, Room 39 and, next to that, the doors to the basement night club Chez Fez. "Here's your room!" Diego cheerfully announces,

pointing at what looks like a wooden door for a cupboard. I think he's joking but surely enough he slides the key in the lock and opens it. In all my times coming to Pikes I've never noticed this door. Room 12 is a hidden gem, right in the very heart of the hotel. It's a trip and stumble away from everything the hotel has to offer. It is absolutely surrounded by the buzz of Pikes. The back terrace on one side, Plaza Mayor and Room 39 on the other and the nightclub Freddie's lies behind its bathroom. It's cool, dark, very spacious and absolutely perfect. I drop my bags, change into shorts and head back to the bar for that drink.

The Pikes pool is nearly three metres deep, and 13 metres long. But no one is ever really there to swim. Sure, as I arrive I witness an eager person doing a length, but as I move closer, she slithers out onto the side and sidles up to the bar to receive an enormous gin and tonic in one silken movement. This is my kind of place, I think to myself for the thousandth time. A red crocodile peeks out over the pool area. It's sitting on the roof of a DJ area, nose just visible to the swimmers it oversees. I wander towards the bar, *cerveza* anticipation at maximum. The bar is painted a deep blue and overlooks the infamous pool seats and Tiki hut that George Michael sat at for the Club Tropicana video. Countless selfies are taken here over the summer as guests recreate it. A quartet of bartenders buzz behind it, preparing drinks, crushing ice, ferrying pool snacks to the guests and dancing to the music. The dub beats I arrived to have sashayed into some classic house and disco. I grab a seat on the south side at the bar. A tall, white stool with a back. Perfect, I think and as I turn around to check out the place I'm interrupted. "That's Tony's seat" says a dark-haired barman with a grin, as he furiously

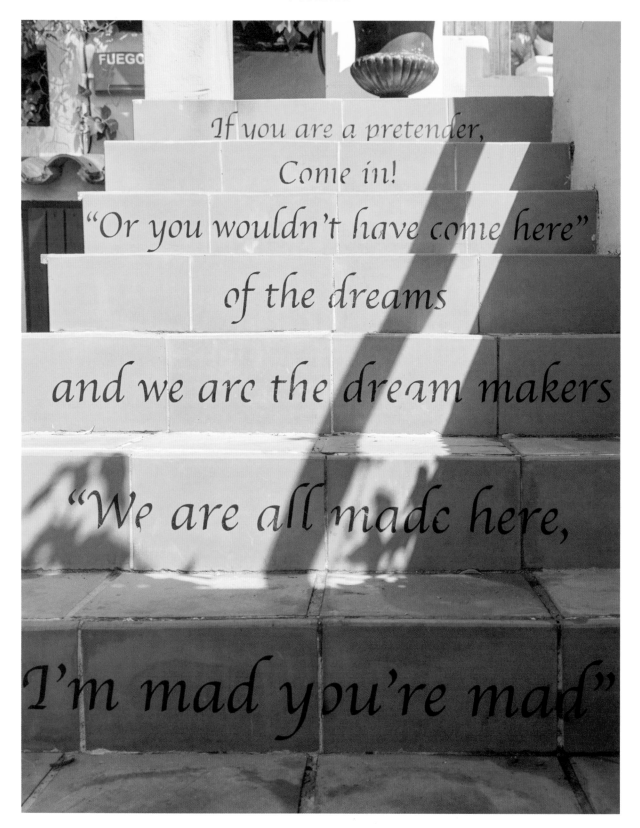

rattles a Boston shaker full of ice. "Oh shit, I'm sorry!" I say in perfect Englishman-abroad style, looking around for the guy whose seat I took. "It's fine," the barman laughs as he pours his concoction into two copa glasses, "but that's where he always sat." Of course he means THE Tony. Pike the raconteur would perch in this very seat while crowds would gather all summer long to listen to him tell tales so impossible they must be true.

Suddenly I feel a little uncomfortable in my chair. I'm not sure I deserve to be sitting in it. I feel the weight of a million tall tales bear down on me as I sit down. I ask the barman if everything I've heard is true. "Probably!" he says, grinning and handing me a frosty beer. It tastes like sweet nectar. I find out this barman is the fabulously named Emil Geronimo and he has been working behind this very bar overlooking the pool for 30 years. He must have seen some sights. Emil's been serving the great and the good for so long he's become an actual part of the place. Even when the season ends he stays on at Pikes and paints the walls and fixes the hotel up. What quickly becomes apparent when you speak to the staff is, that, for many of them, leaving Pikes is not an option. They are a part of it and it is a part of them. And maybe that's one of the ingredients of what makes this place so special. Every one of the staff you meet feels like they couldn't fit in anywhere else. They all play a crucial part in keeping the hotel ticking along and each play a leading role in the neverending play that is Pikes Hotel. Whether it's booking the DJs, serving behind the bar, organising events, cleaning the rooms, cutting the grass, cooking in the kitchen, waiting the tables, managing the night-time escapades, or hosting their own boudoir and ball-pool jacuzzi karaoke room, they all add something unique to the hotel. As Emil moves away from me to serve another

guest, I turn my back to his bar and drink in the scene, and beer, before me. Things are the very definition of lounging. All shapes and sizes of people are sprawled on sun loungers and chairs. There are few better places to have a hangover. People are laughing and chatting across the terrace. They're smoking, checking last night's Instagram, the dub beats and the sun's heat are making everybody's bones heavy and there's no reason to move.

A holler from the terrace grabs my attention – two guys saunter into view who look like they've had quite the night. They're both tall, good looking and are sporting the big grins of a pair who've got a story they can't wait to tell. They look like they've been wearing their sunglasses for at least 24 hours... They make a beeline for a man and woman who are wearing matching cowboy hats and entwined on a lounger. The couple unwind from each other and leap up to high five and hug the pair of reprobates like old friends. "They only met last night," a lady with impeccable hair and make-up and wearing a man's pinstriped shirt over a neon orange bikini says to me. She pauses to take a glug from her gin and tonic. "They seem to know that couple pretty well" I reply. "No, all of them" she corrects me. "I mean obviously the couple know each other but those two guys only met each other last night. They bonded at the bar as they're both doctors. One of them's Dutch and the other's from London. The London one is also my husband – I was wondering where he'd got to. I don't think either of them have been to bed." Her husband is now heading in our direction. He gives his wife an enormous kiss, shakes my hand and they wander up to the restaurant, hand in hand. I scan the cocktail list and ask Emil for a Tony's Tales. Well, you would, wouldn't you?

MARGARITA

This is the best way to drink this classic
cocktail in our opinion. If made correctly,
the fresh ice maintains the drinks potential
and temperature so you can take your time to
enjoy it, even under the hot Ibizan sun.

Ingredients	How to make
Silver tequila 60 ml/2 fl.oz. Cointreau 40 ml/1/2 fl.oz. Lime juice 20 ml/3/4 fl.oz. Salt for rimming glass (optional) Cubed ice Garnish: Lime wheel	Build the ingredients in the glass of a Boston shaker and add cubed ice. Cover with the shaker, shake and strain into a salt-rimmed rocks glass, if desired. Add fresh cubed ice, garnish as shown and serve straightaway.

Serves 1

TEEN SPIRIT

This Tiki-style cocktail promotes alcohol-free
spirit that in the case of the non-alcoholic
rum used here adds a noticeable woody acidity.
This combines beautifully with the fruit and
the herbaceous nature of the falernum syrup.
A cocktail experience that's hangover free.

Ingredients

Non-alcoholic rum
50 ml/1 2/3 fl.oz.
Falernum syrup
25 ml/1 fl.oz.
Lime juice
15 ml/1/2 fl.oz.
Coconut cream
50 ml/1 2/3 fl.oz.
Pineapple juice
100 ml/3 1/3 fl.oz.
Cubed ice
Garnish: Pineapple
wedge and leaf,
edible flowers

Serves 1

How to make

Add all the ingredients
to a cocktail shaker.
Add cubed ice, shake
well and strain over
a Tiki mug or highball
glass filled with fresh
cubed ice. Garnish
as shown and serve
straightaway.

COSMIC PINEAPPLE

Ingredients

Mezcal
40 ml/1 1/2 fl.oz.
Cointreau
20 ml/3/4 fl.oz.
Grilled Pineapple Purée
(see #note)
50 ml/1 2/3 fl.oz.
Agave syrup
15 ml/1/2 fl.oz.
Lime juice
20 ml/3/4 fl. oz.
Chilli tincture
Cubed ice
Garnish: Pineapple
wedge, crushed pink
peppercorns

Serves 1

How to make

Add all the ingredients
to a cocktail shaker
with 2 drops of chilli
tincture. Add cubed
ice and shake hard.
Double strain into an
ice-filled rocks glass,
garnish as shown and
serve straightaway.

#note: To make Grilled
Pineapple Purée, grill
8 slices of pineapple
for 5 minutes on each
side, until browning
and tender. Purée in
a blender, strain
and chill in fridge
until needed.

RABBIT'S REVENGE & GINGER SPICE

Without doubt the best way to deliver goodness
to your body is with ressed and extracted juices,
particularly the vegetable ones. They facilitate
the absorption of vitamins and minerals in the
most enjoyable way possible. Just holding one of
these bad boys gives a feeling of wellness and is
the perfect antidote for what you did last night.
That's right, we saw you.

Ingredients

Rabbit's Revenge:
1 Raw beetroot
2 Celery sticks
1 Green apple
Carrots (to add bulk)
Crushed ice
Garnish: Celery stick,
beetroot sprouts

Ginger Spice:
2 Green Apples, we use
Golden Delicious
1/2 Thumb-size fresh
ginger piece
Carrots (to add bulk)
Crushed ice
Garnish: Apple fan,
ginger slice, carrot
shaving

Each recipe serves 1

How to make

Both drinks are made
using the same method,
as follows: pass all
the ingredients through
a juice extractor.
Pour the liquid gently
into a hurricane glass
containing a little
crushed ice, holding
back the surface foam
on the juice as much
as possible. Garnish
as shown and serve
straightaway.

#note: Use fridge-cold
fruit and veg to give
a refreshingly cold
drink that requires
absolutely minimal ice.

PUNKA COLADA

Ingredients

White rum
50 ml/1 2/3 fl.oz.
Coconut cream
50 ml/1 2/3 fl.oz.
Pineapple juice
50 ml/1 2/3 fl.oz.
10 Pineapple chunks
Crushed ice
Garnish: Pineapple
wedge and leaf,
Maraschino cherry

Serves 1

How to make

Add all the ingredients
plus 1/2 a scoop of
crushed ice to a
blender and blend
until smooth. Pour
into a hurricane glass,
garnish as shown, and
serve straightaway.

WHAM!

Ingredients

Coconut cream
50 ml/1 2/3 fl.oz.
Mango purée
50 ml/1 2/3 fl.oz.
Orange juice
150 ml/5 fl.oz.
6 Pineapple chunks
2 tbsps Frozen fruits
of the forest (berries)
1/2 Banana
Sugar syrup (optional)
Crushed ice
Garnish: Pineapple
wedge, frozen berries,
mint sprig

Serves 1

How to make

Add all the ingredients
to a blender with 1/2
a scoop of crushed ice
and blend until smooth.
Add sugar syrup to
taste (if desired).
Pour into a hurricane
glass and add a little
crushed ice. Garnish
as shown and serve
straightaway.

MONKEY'S MOJITO

Ingredients

White rum
50 ml/1 2/3 fl.oz.
Sugar syrup
25 ml/1 fl.oz.
Soda water
40 ml/1 1/2 fl.oz.
1 Lime, quartered
10 Mint leaves
Crushed ice
Garnish: Mint sprig,
lime slice

Serves 1

How to make

Muddle the lime
quarters and sugar
syrup in a highball
glass. Add the mint
leaves and bruise
gently (try not to
smash or tear them).
Add the rum and
stir with a barspoon.
Leaving the spoon in
the glass, add 1/2 a
scoop of crushed ice
and stir again. Add
soda and stir. Top
up with crushed ice,
garnish as shown and
serve straightaway.

CLUB TROPICANA

Despite the persistent rumours, unfortunately, this drink isn't free. Everything about this cocktail makes sense - rum and pineapple, pineapple and coconut, vanilla and orange, citrus and sweet, wood and fruit. Our serving suggestion is to sip it while at Pikes, sitting by our iconic pool.

Ingredients

White rum
15 ml/1/2 fl.oz.
Dark rum
20 ml/3/4 fl.oz.
Vanilla vodka
15 ml/1/2 fl.oz.
Cointreau
10 ml/1/3 fl.oz.
Coconut cream
50 ml/1 2/3 fl.oz.
Orange juice
75 ml/2 1/2 fl.oz.
4 pineapple chunks
Lime juice
Garnish: Pineapple wedge, orange slices, mint sprig

Serves 1

How to make

Add all the ingredients to a blender with a dash of lime juice and add 1/2 a scoop of crushed ice. Blend well. Add a little crushed ice to a double rocks glass (or George Michael swimwear vessel!) and fill with the drink. Top with more crushed ice (if necessary), garnish as shown and serve straightaway.

DOWN THE RABBIT HOLE

We prefer to use kombucha that's brewed here in Ibiza as the effervescent element to this drink. Its natural fermentation brings something of a pH element to a drink that would normally boast acidity. In fact, we suggest you use kombucha as an alternative to carbonated soft drinks at any opportunity.

Ingredients

Vodka
45 ml/1 3/4 fl.oz.
Elderflower liqueur
15 ml/1/2 fl.oz.
Lemon juice
15 ml/1/2 fl.oz.
Ginger syrup
10 ml/1/3 fl.oz.
Kombucha to top up
Cubed ice
Garnish: Fresh ginger slice, lemon wheel, sprig of foraged flora

Serves 1

How to make

Add all the ingredients to a cocktail shaker. Half-fill with cubed ice and shake. Add fresh cubed ice to a highball glass. Strain the drink into the glass. Top up with kombucha, garnish as shown and serve straightaway.

Tony's Tale #1

There's nothing cliquier than the music business and it was the Club Tropicana video for Wham! brought me into that world.

George Michael came and stayed first of all in the early days when I only had six rooms, so he would have been in one of those ones. I don't know much about music and when they were here it was all rough cane and cacti – it was a bit of a shithouse with a 500-year-old building. I was sitting here and a guy walked up and asked if I was the owner. He said he worked for a company looking for spots to film music videos and that he was representing Wham! and he thought it was an ideal location. I didn't know then who Wham! or George Michael were. Artists like Five

Star and Boy George also came to stay at Pikes, and Spandau Ballet came here as kids when they were signed to Chrysalis Records. The record company took the rooms in my hotel and put the guys in a place up the hill somewhere. The band came down and saw us all sitting around the pool having drinks and weren't too happy about it; their place was a building site. Tony Hadley and the rest demanded the record company swap with them. They didn't...

After a few days the head of Chrysalis Records bought my car off me...

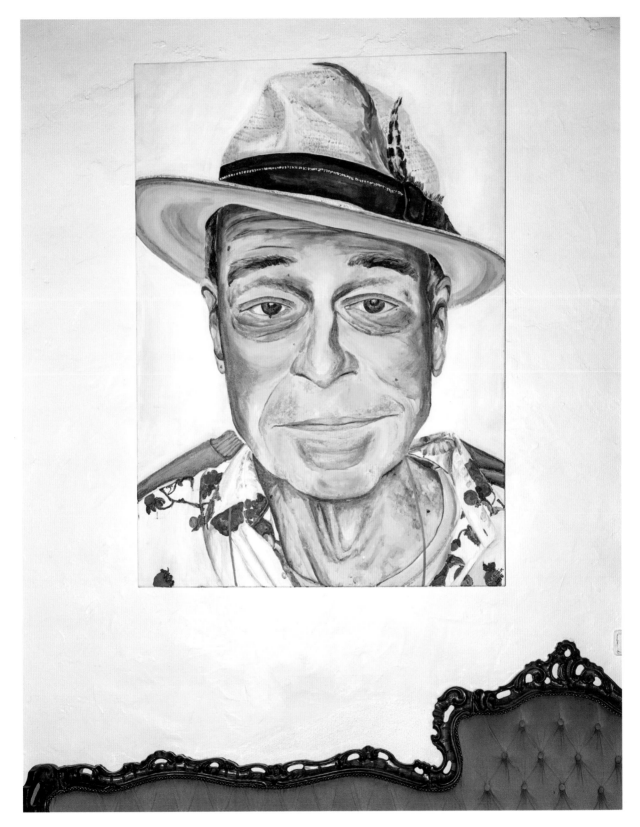

There are fewer things more Ibizan than basking in the sun, sitting with friends and sipping chilled drinks during the day. I've made my way up the stairs and, as lunch approaches, the tables and chairs of the Room 39 restaurant have started to fill up. Waves of laughter and clinking glasses join the soundtrack to the hotel. The atmosphere feels like it's starting to nudge up, just a little bit, just as the buttons on the Hawaiian shirts are gradually coming undone.

People are getting lubricated by more than the Factor 20 sunscreen and have decided it's probably time for a change of scene from the pool. Eating definitely isn't cheating here. Crisp white wines have been ordered to go with the fresh and vibrant salads (for those keeping things healthy), and the chunky burgers (for those wanting something a bit denser as they look ahead to the evening) and people are starting to think about cocktails.

Room 39 is blue-walled, with two walls that overlook the pool, which maximise any breeze for the guests that sit on blue leather chairs around the black glass-topped tables. All along the back wall runs a bar and behind that, hanging from virtually every surface is some kind of curio – a huge plaster nose sticks out from behind a pillar. Who knows what that's a reference to? A blue plaque proclaiming The Man Who Slept With Your Wife Lives Here is just behind me, while another one on the side of the room retorts with The Woman Who Slept With Your Husband Lives Here. I'm guessing that's where the name for the Home Of The Adultress cocktail comes from. A pair of porcelain pugs guard the shelves of spirit bottles, while a black china stallion stares up at a painting of a dancer that I assume

must be the inspiration for the Prima Ballerina cocktail. I've been in some hotels where it's weird when you're on your own in the bar or restaurant. Waiters either fuss over you constantly or ignore your existence, but it's not like that here in Room 39 – the beautifully tattooed bar and waiting staff look effortlessly cool in their silk shirt uniforms and create the drinks orders and bring your food with a warm, genuine smile. They don't just drop off the food and drinks and go either, they stay and chat for a while.

It's genre-bending, dubstep pioneering DJ, Pikes regular and bon viveur Artwork says, "It's totally the opposite of going to a club. You could 100% turn up there on your own. I wouldn't want to go to Amnesia on my own and wander about. But you know you could go to Pikes on your own, get a drink and just sit down and the next thing you know you'll be talking to someone who could be anyone. It could be someone who's 22 years old or a prince who's 70 years old. It could be absolutely anyone and I think that's the magical thing about it. It is like the weirdest house party you've ever been to in your life. Pikes is my favourite place to play on earth. People love music there and they are there more for the atmosphere of the place and less to go and see a particular DJ like you would in a nondescript club that could be anywhere in the world. And you go there for the atmosphere of being at Pikes. People there are very, very open to you playing whatever you want to do, whatever you think that they want on that night. It's not like going to do a festival set where people expect you to go and play your thing and fit into a box. At Pikes you can do whatever you want and go completely where you like. And the people there will go along with it. I genuinely don't leave the place once I'm here. I do have plans – people invite me down to their

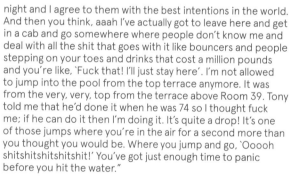

night and I agree to them with the best intentions in the world. And then you think, aaah I've actually got to leave here and get in a cab and go somewhere where people don't know me and deal with all the shit that goes with it like bouncers and people stepping on your toes and drinks that cost a million pounds and you're like, 'Fuck that! I'll just stay here'. I'm not allowed to jump into the pool from the top terrace anymore. It was from the very, very, top from the terrace above Room 39. Tony told me that he'd done it when he was 74 so I thought fuck me; if he can do it then I'm doing it. It's quite a drop! It's one of those jumps where you're in the air for a second more than you thought you would be. Where you jump and go, 'Ooooh shitshitshitshitshit!' You've got just enough time to panic before you hit the water."

I mention this to the waitress as she brings me a Honey Dijon and she laughs saying she remembers when he did it. Then, the man on the table next to me leans over. "It's [pool] water that never seems to warm up," he exclaims. "It goes against the laws of physics!" Introducing himself as Warren, my new conversation partner is a burly bald guy who I soon find out flits between being an architect and a shaman. Of course he does... and it transpires that he's seen the highs and the lows of the place. "I've been coming to Pikes for 22 years, if that doesn't give away my age too much," he says before pouring me a glass of his Sangria and bringing me into his conversation. "For me I felt like I was stepping up a bit from the San Antonio scene and it felt a bit posh. A bit posh and very wild... but back then it was just like today in that you can come here on your own and, within a couple of hours, find yourself chatting to everyone around the pool. You never know who you're going to meet. I will always know people down here. It's my kind of

social club. My British Legion. You often find in other hotels that they almost have a signature profile of clients, but it's a real mash-up of people here – in every sense of the word."

"I'd come and stay and watch my friends DJ here and then nine years ago I moved to Ibiza, which meant I didn't really come to Pikes much for a couple of years. It's good to have been witness to the full journey of Pikes; I was here when it was in its first kind of pomp. Then it went a bit downhill; when you came here it was a bit sad. Tony, of course, was always entertaining and a great guy but it was sad to see the place start to nosedive. The atmosphere wasn't the same any more. It's great to see the place buzzing again. It seems to have evolved quite naturally over the years since Andy and Dawn took it over. The place has got its character back again. What's quite funny is that I've got memories of every single room – ones I'm not going to recount to you!" It needs to be mentioned that Warren is accompanied by two women, one wearing a diamanté swimming costume with gold epaulettes and the other a purple feather skirt. They look fantastic. "Might be a bit much for lunch," they both laugh, "but we're heading somewhere after this and well, why not?"

"Well, why not" seems to be an underlying theme to Pikes. A lot of people find when they get here that they feel completely at home. People can wander in after being away for as long as five years and be greeted spontaneously like a long-lost brother or sister and like they were there just last week. I sit back and finish my glass of cold Sangria – enjoying the fact that the warmth of the Ibizan sun on my face is matched by the warmth of the hospitality and the new friends I've just made.

DOUBLE CLAP

Those within ear shot of a Tony Pike story would also have been witness to his infamous double clap. On delivery of the punch line, Tony would reinforce it with a loud double clap and flash a cheeky smile. Our double clap cocktail has an Asian vibe, marrying spice, sweet, fruit and herb notes and tequila adds the spirit bite. This cocktail is brave and complex and exotic.

Ingredients

Tequila
60 ml/2 fl.oz.
Coconut syrup
20 ml/3/4 fl.oz.
Lime juice
7.5 ml/1/6 fl.oz.
Yuzu juice
7.5 ml/1/6 fl.oz
Orange juice
10 ml/1/3 fl.oz.
Pineapple juice
15 ml/1/2 fl.oz.
Soda water
25 ml/1 fl.oz.
Lemongrass piece
Fresh ginger piece
1/2 Small red chilli
Coriander sprig
Cubed ice
Garnish: Fresh ginger slice, small red chilli, coriander sprig, lemon slice

Serves 1

How to make

Muddle the chilli with the lemongrass, ginger and coriander in a cocktail shaker. Add the tequila, all the citrus juices, the pineapple juice and the coconut syrup. Add cubed ice and shake hard. Strain into a highball glass filled with fresh cubed ice. Top up with chilled soda, garnish as shown and serve straightaway.

CLASS OF 39

Ingredients

Gin
50 ml /1 2/3 fl.oz.
Passoa
15 ml/1/2 fl.oz.
10 ml/1/3 fl oz.
Sugar syrup
1 Passion fruit
6-8 Basil leaves
Basil sparkling water
to top up
Cubed and crushed ice
Garnish: Passion fruit
wheel, basil leaf

Serves 1

How to make

Cut a wheel from the
end off the passion
fruit and reserve to
garnish. Scoop the
seeds from the rest
of the fruit into a
cocktail shaker. Add
the basil leaves and
muddle. Add the gin,
passoa and sugar syrup
and half-fill with cubed
ice. Shake hard and
double strain into a
highball glass filled
with crushed ice. Top
up with basil sparkling
water, garnish as shown
and serve straightaway.

SANGRIA

The classic Spanish summertime refreshment. Red *Sangria* is still the winner in our eyes although *Sangria de Cava* is not far behind. Choose quality base liquor, a nice fruity red wine, freshly squeeze your juice and use local seasonal fruit to garnish. Stir ingredients lovingly and serve cold.

Ingredients

1/2 Green apple
1/2 Peach
1/2 Orange
1/2 Lemon
Brandy
60 ml/2 fl.oz.
Cointreau (or other orange liqueur)
40 ml/1 1/2 fl.oz.
Orange juice
150 ml/5 fl.oz.
Peach juice
50 ml/1 2/3 fl.oz.
750-ml Bottle quality Spanish red wine (such as Garnacha), chilled
Sugar syrup
50 ml/1 2/3 fl.oz.
Cubed ice
Frozen fruits of the forest (berries)

Serves 4

How to make

Slice and/or chop the fruit. Combine it with all the other ingredients in a large jug. Add a little cubed ice and 2 tablespoons frozen fruits of the forest to maintain a chill in the Sangria, stir and serve in ice-filled wine glasses.

#Note 1: Add extra ice to the glasses, not to the jug. It should be ice free to avoid watering down.

#Note 2: Sangria is always better if you allow the fruit to steep in the Brandy and liqueur overnight.

DIRTY DEEDS DAIQUIRI

The frozen strawberry Daiquiri is the most popular cocktail at Pikes. The daily battle between bar and heat means that anything frozen at anytime is an ally. We use frozen strawberries in our Daiquiri, which means we reduce ice and means we can deliver maximum flavour and strength in the cocktail so guests can enjoy a cold drink that's stronger for longer.

Ingredients

White rum
50 ml/1 2/3 fl.oz.
Lime juice
20 ml/3/4 fl. oz.
Sugar syrup
25 ml/1 fl.oz.
10 Frozen strawberries
Crushed ice
Garnish: Lime twist

Serves 1

How to make

Add all the ingredients to a blender and blend until smooth. Add 1 scoop of crushed ice and blend until you have an icy slush. Pour the drink into a large, chilled wine glass, garnish as shown and serve straightaway.

SUNDAY ROAST

Based on a classic Bloody Mary you'd have at
a Pikes roast, we added carrot juice to soften
the acidity of the tomato, and potato vodka and a
homemade green bean syrup to add authenticity. The
usual Mary condiments give depth. Although this is
most certainly a vegetarian roast, you could add
a spoon of Bovril if you prefer it a bit beefy.

Ingredients

Potato vodka
50 ml/1 2/3 fl.oz.
Manzanilla sherry
15 ml/1/2 fl.oz.
Lemon juice
15 ml/1/2 fl.oz.
Tomato juice
70 ml/2 1/4 fl.oz.
Carrot juice
60 ml/2 fl.oz.
Green Bean Syrup
(see #note)
15 ml/1/2 fl.oz.
Tabasco sauce
Worcestershire sauce
Salt and black pepper
Cubed ice
Garnish: Carrot slice,
carrot tops, green
bean, lemon slice

Serves 1

How to make

Build the ingredients
in a Boston shaker,
adding 2 dashes each of
the sauces and season.
Add 1/2 a scoop of
cubed ice then pour
the liquid into the
Boston glass and back
into the shaker again
and repeat a few times.
Add fresh cubed ice to
a large highball glass
and strain the drink
into it. Garnish as
shown, add a grind of
black pepper and serve
straightaway.

#note: To make Green
Bean Syrup, heat
155 g/3/4 cup sugar
with 155 ml/2/3 cup
cold water in a small
saucepan, until clear
and syrupy. Steam
250 g/9 oz. beans for
3-4 minutes only. Purée
them in a blender with
the syrup (you should
have 250 ml/1 cup),
strain and keep in the
fridge for 3-4 days.

PIKES RUM PUNCH

Created for our friend George from Nightmares
On Wax, we knew this cocktail needed authenticity
in ingredients and to have a spicy bite but also
the spirit burn to boot. This clove and pink
peppercorn-laced combination of rums is delicately
balanced with fresh pineapple and lime and is the
perfect way to kick start the night.

Ingredients

Premium white rum
25 ml/1 fl.oz.
Premium Jamaican rum
25 ml/1 fl.oz.
Lime juice
20 ml/3/4 fl.oz.
Pineapple juice
25 ml/1 fl.oz.
Pink peppercorn syrup
25 ml/1 fl.oz.
8 Cloves
Overproof rum to float
Soda water to top up
Cubed ice
Garnish: Peppercorn
sprig (optional),
clove-studded fresh
ginger slice

Serves 1

How To Make

Muddle the cloves
in a cocktail shaker.
Add the rum, pink
peppercorn syrup and
the lime and pineapple
juices. Add cubed ice,
shake very well and
double strain into an
ice-filled double-rocks
glass. Top up with soda
water (leaving space
for the rum) and add
a float of overproof
rum to finish. Garnish
as shown and serve
straightaway.

MR WHIPPY

Ingredients

Premium pisco (steep 15
coffee Beans in it for
5 minutes before using)
40 ml/1 1/2 fl.oz.
Crème de cacao blanc
25 ml/1 fl.oz.
Lemon juice
20 ml/3/4 fl. oz.
Sugar syrup
20 ml/3/4 fl. oz
1/2 Avocado
Cubed ice
Garnish: Chilli powder,
salt flakes for rimming
glass (optional)

Serves 1

How to make

Add the avocado flesh,
crème de cacao blanc,
lemon juice, pisco
and sugar syrup to a
blender. Blend until
liquid. Rim a coupe
glass with the chilli
and salt mix (if
desired) and put it
in the fridge to chill.
Pour the drink from the
blender into a cocktail
shaker and add cubed
ice. Shake hard, strain
gently into the chilled
and rimmed coupe and
serve straightaway.

Tony's Tale #2

One of the best things that ever happened to me was when Joan Baez walked in, she was a good-looking woman. When Joan Baez was here she sang some impromptu songs during dinner in the courtyard and led me, plus 50 or 60 diners, down to the pool where we danced until the sun came up. It was one of my favourite ever nights at Pikes.

She said it was because the place was so magical; I told her it was her voice that had entranced everyone. I took her out for lunch and she did a drawing of her driving the boat and me standing behind her, holding her...

I remember a long time ago, the band Yes were staying here. I came back from the clubs at about 4am and they were all sitting around smoking dope.

There was a bit of an electrical storm that night and when I said hello they all told me to be quiet because a spaceship was going to land. They'd been watching it for hours and didn't know if there was intelligent life was on board.

They were staring at a light on top of a telegraph pole so I left them to it.

Afternoon Tea

Right up above everything, looking down on the rest of the hotel is the top terrace. It's the place the DJ Artwork, and a number of other guests, have jumped into the pool from and it's here I climb up several flights of steps to meet Dawn Hindle, Creative Director of Pikes for that most English of things – afternoon tea.

Which sounds ridiculous, it's Ibiza, 36 degrees and the heat's making the fields in the distance wobble. It's something you might expect at the Savoy or Ritz Hotel in London, but cream teas might get a bit sweaty under a sweltering sun. Luckily, as well as being the highest point of the hotel, the upper terrace is one of the shadiest too (not including Sunny's Boudoir – more on that later). Rattan blinds lie across wooden beams to create a very welcome retreat from the blazing sun. Its elevated position means you catch a constant breeze and the sounds of an entire hotel enjoying itself rise up from below. It's from here that you realise how far you are from clichéd Ibiza. There's no other hotel in sight – just flood plains reaching to the hills on one side and San Antonio and its beaches in the far distance on the other.

The tables are covered in starched white tablecloths and folded napkins. Sitting at one of them is Pikes co-owner and Creative Director, Dawn Hindle. With a shock of black and white hair and a razor blade necklace, she is the epitome of rock 'n' roll. She's from Stockport and her Northern manners haven't left her after all these years in Ibiza. She's holding a china teapot, already pouring tea into a dainty cup for me, and seems oblivious to the heat. As founder of cult club monolith Manumission and also cult youth hotel, Ibiza Rocks, she really is an integral part of the island's musical history.

The decision to buy Pikes came from seeing it in the doldrums and realising that she and co-founder of Manumission and Ibiza Rocks, Andy McKay, needed to step in to both preserve the legendary hotel and nudge it forward without changing the magic found in it.

Dawn welcomes me with a massive hug and a trademark cackle as she tells me the teas are only really for show – she's already ordered us some proper drinks, designed especially to be drunk up here with the petit fours and sandwiches with crusts cut off. She's excited that the hotel is now in the position to be able to start increasing its cocktail offerings to things like this. It's worth remembering that when the main building was built, the Ibizans weren't really thinking about footfall and bar wait times. But making wholesale changes is not the Pikes way, and ripping out walls and remodelling bits would lose some of the Pikes charm. The past 11 years have actually involved lots of changes, but ones that were not so obvious to a guests eye. It's only in the last two summers that they've been able to really focus on levelling up both the drinks and the food at the place. This is something they've done with Dawn's Curiosity Shop concept. In the close season, Dawn spends a lot of time travelling and visiting fleamarkets and vintage sales, picking up the weird ephemera that you find around Pikes. These curiosities are the inspirations behind many of the names you'll find on the Pikes cocktail list, and in this book.

The Curiosity Shop isn't really a physical thing. It's a flighty concept that flits between Room 39 after dinner's been served, the bar on the back terrace and also a tiny shed that opens up to reveal a fully stocked cocktail bar and has appeared in various places around the hotel. It currently

resides not far from Sunny's Boudoir, near the entrance to the back terrace.

"In 2018, we started the Curiosity Shop cocktail concept," Dawn says, "and from there have created a range of cocktails using a collection of lost and found objects I've come across around the world as inspiration. The whole back terrace is now dedicated to cocktails so it's been great to be heading in a new direction with that. It's only been the last couple of years that we've got a strong identity of what the restaurant really represented. That was Lee and Steve's vision and this year we've embraced a lot more of that English element of what we're doing so it's all about locally-sourced produce and English ideas with a twist. Because what we're doing here is working, we've really established Pikes as a unique little part of Ibiza and it represents to me a lot of what Ibiza has been for us throughout the 23 years that we've been here.

It's quite a significant part of the Ibizan landscape and that comes together from a lot of little strings that attach all these cultural things: music, food, drink and everything else we do. We've really embraced Pikes' authenticity and what it means to the island, the people on it and not only its regulars but people who are experiencing it for the first time. It is a special and unique part of the island that we've taken on – I look at it like an old piece of art that we've tried to restore and to regenerate." As if on cue, Will Miles, the Pikes pastry chef and mastermind behind the afternoon tea concept appears with our traditional three-tiered cake stand festooned with deliciously delicate cakes and finger sandwiches. He's closely followed by a waiter bearing a tray that brings us a Pikes G&Tea and a Grass is Greener cocktails as refreshing pick-me-ups.

"We're now in a position where not only has Pikes come back to life but I think it's definitely more successful than it's ever been in its whole history. Our whole thing is about preservation of the building and with part of the ethos that we've tried to create is that we're just relaxing into letting Pikes live itself in a really natural way so we're not forcing anything onto it.

What makes Pikes special is all the people that work here and also the people it attracts. It's something that goes back to the family ethos that we have. The staff really do feel like one big family and the people who come to stay with us feel like they're part of that extended family. I think that's what makes everything click here. With Pikes I do loads of collaborations and the place really is a sum of its parts. Every year we work with new people who genuinely love the place and by working with them we get to retain a little essence of them each time.

For instance, people like Starlover this year who have given us pieces of artwork (and the awesome leather jacket photographed for page 1 of this book) and photographer Diana Gomez, who did an open air exhibition here and has left a piece of her art at the bottom of the swimming pool. Or the artist Rory Dobner who left his mark on all the walls, whether it's the room numbers, singing chameleon or Cheshire cat... This place is a tapestry and each year the fabric gets richer because it builds up and builds on. It keeps organically growing and the concept gets stronger. I think part of the thing with Pikes is to really maintain the heritage and I want to keep that idiosyncratic feel. I think it's about layering it up rather than stripping it back – more is more... Just like make up."

GRASS IS GREENER

Here is a cocktail designed to suit our afternoon tea. The key objectives for this were fresh, cooling, fruity, floral, and all of these come through in this gin-based cocktail. Dessert wine, elderflower liqueur and limoncello all play a part in this potent up-drink. The muddled basil gives the drink a lovely freshness and its distinctive pale green colouring.

Ingredients

Gin
30 ml/1 fl.oz.
Dessert wine
15 ml/1/2 fl.oz.
Elderflower liqueur
10 ml/1/3 fl.oz.
Limoncello
5 ml/1/6 fl.oz.
Lime juice
20 ml/3/4 fl.oz.
Vanilla syrup
10 ml/1/3 fl.oz.
6 Basil leaves
Lime bitters
White pepper
Cubed ice
Garnish: Basil leaf

Serves 1

How to make

Muddle the basil leaves in a cocktail shaker, then add all the other ingredients plus a dash of the bitters and a pinch of pepper. Add cubed ice, shake hard and double strain into a chilled coupe or martini glass. Garnish as shown and serve straightaway.

THE PROVOCATEUR

Ingredients

Vanilla vodka
50 ml/1 2/3 fl.oz.
Pink grapefruit juice
15 ml/1/2 fl.oz.
Lemon juice
10 ml/1/3 fl.oz.
Peach syrup
10 ml/1/3 fl.oz.
Blood orange syrup
5 ml/1/6 fl.oz.
Cava to top up
Cubed ice
Garnish: Dehydrated
orange wheel and edible
flowers

Serves 1

How to make

Add the vanilla vodka,
pink grapefruit juice,
lemon juice and syrups
to a cocktail shaker.
Shake and strain over
a large wine glass
filled with cubed ice.
Top up with chilled
cava. Garnish as shown
and serve straightaway.

FINGER ON THE TRIGGER

Ingredients

Gin
40 ml/1 1/2 fl.oz.
Elderflower liqueur
20 ml/3/4 fl.oz.
Apple juice
20 ml/3/4 fl.oz.
Lemon juice
15 ml/1/2 fl.oz.
1/2 Thumb-size cucumber
piece
Small thyme sprig
Rosemary sparkling
water to top up
Cubed and crushed ice
Garnish: Cucumber
strip, thyme sprig

Serves 1

How to make

Muddle the cucumber
well in a cocktail
shaker, add the thyme
sprig and muddle again.
Add the gin, elderflower
liqueur, apple and
lemon juices. Add cubed
ice, shake and double
strain into a highball
glass filled with
crushed ice. Top up
with rosemary sparkling
water, stir, garnish
as shown and serve
straightaway.

PIKEY BLINDER

This Champagne-based cocktail is surprisingly refreshing and leans on local fruit to bring a moreish fruit and citrus depth. Adding oleo-saccharum lifts this cocktail from a simple kir royale style to an even more regal experience "by order of the Pikey f··kin' blinders!"

Ingredients

Oleo-saccharum, chilled
(see #note)
5 ml/1/6 fl.oz.
Crème de mure
20 ml/3/4 fl.oz.
Champagne to top up
Cubed ice
Garnish: Lemon twist,
frozen blackberries
or blackcurrants

Serves 1

How to make

Add the oleo-saccharum and créme de mure to a chilled flute, pouring over an ice cube. Top up with Champagne, garnish as shown and serve straightaway.

#note: To make Oleo-saccharum, use 3:1 ratio citrus peel to caster/superfine sugar. Peel 1 medium-large firm-skinned (unwaxed) lemon, leaving all the white pith behind. Add the peel to a clean sealable jar, followed by 1/3 the volume of peel of sugar. Shake and turn the jar, then refrigerate it for 12-24 hours. Pass the mixture through a funnel to strain off the sweetened citrus oils; this is your Oleo-saccharum. Kept refrigerated, it will keep for 4-5 days.

PIKES G&TEA

When you visit Room 39 you can't help but notice the enchanting perfume of the jasmine bush. The Pikes G&Tea is inspired by this: mixing jasmine syrup, local lemon juice and jasmine tea to elaborate on a classic gin and tonic for an experience of something that is quintessentially Anglo-cencan.

Ingredients

Gin
50 ml/1 2/3 fl.oz.
Lemon juice
5 ml/1/6 fl.oz.
Jasmine syrup
20 ml/3/4 fl.oz.
Jasmine tea, cooled
40 ml/1 1/2 fl.oz.
Tonic water to top up
Cubed ice
Garnish: Lemon slice, jasmine flowers

Serves 1

How to make

Add the gin, jasmine syrup, cold jasmine tea and lemon juice to a shaker. Add cubed ice, shake and strain into a highball or large wine glass filled with fresh cubed ice. Top up with tonic water. Garnish as shown and serve straightaway.

MY TAI TEMPTATION

Though based around the classic recipe, our Mai Tai is influenced by local produce. We insist on fresh ingredients and a quality base liquor but we have added a touch of pomegranate syrup to create an even fruitier depth. Keep it fun, and choose something interesting to serve it in.

Ingredients

White rum
25 ml/1 fl.oz.
Dark rum
25 ml/1 fl.oz.
Cointreau
15 ml/1/2 fl.oz.
Lime juice
30 ml/1 fl.oz.
Orgeat syrup
10 ml/1/3 fl.oz.
Pomegranate syrup
5 ml/1/6 fl.oz.
Cubed and crushed ice
Garnish: Caramelized pineapple wedge, orange wedge, pomegranate seeds, mint sprig

Serves 1

How to make

Build all of the ingredients in a cocktail shaker. Add cubed ice, shake and strain into a rocks glass (or your chosen vessel!) filled with crushed ice. Garnish as shown and serve straightaway.

THE
MANSFIELD

This is inspired by our in-house rock star hairdresser, Lyndell Mansfield. Her everything-pink attitude shows that hairdressers on tour never bore. This summery up-drink is a balance of fruity and citrus. The egg white adds a creamy texture and a pale pink bouffant makes it look like it's definitely had the Mansfield treatment.

Ingredients

Vodka
60 ml/2 fl.oz.
Lemon juice
20 ml/3/4 fl.oz.
Egg white
20 ml/3/4 fl.oz.
Lime cordial
10 ml/1/3 fl.oz.
Elderflower syrup
15 ml/1/2 fl.oz.
4 Fresh raspberries
Rhubarb bitters
Cubed ice
Garnish: Dehydrated
or fresh raspberries

Serves 1

How to make

Muddle the raspberries in a cocktail shaker, add the egg white and dry shake (i.e. without ice). Add all of the other ingredients plus a dash of the bitters along with cubed ice and shake well. Double strain into a chilled coupe glass, garnish as shown and serve straightaway.

Tony's Tale #3

Jon Bon Jovi was fantastic when he was here; he's a lovely guy. We had all of Bon Jovi staying here at the same time as Tony Curtis, who was in Room 26 with his wife.

Tony was a very friendly guy; he tried to borrow my car but I wouldn't lend it to him because I thought if he goes out, has a drink and crashes it then I've had it. So he asked me if I could get him a convertible. I had a scout around and managed to find him a Ford Escort two-seater convertible. He got in the car with his wife and he asked me to join them. There weren't any other seats so I had to sit on the back. He had a pair of racing gloves, which he took forever to put on. I asked him why he was taking so long. He replied "I'm just reminiscing – four things have happened today that have never happened to me before: I found an island I didn't know existed, I found a hotel that I love that I didn't know existed, I've made a new friend in you who I didn't know existed and I'm with my lovely wife who I

love so much because she saved me from peril. She's been my rock and I love her to bits." We went out for lunch and it was very, very nice and Tony was so hospitable.

I was in talks at the time with a very rich Russian to sell him Pikes for about £3m, and one day Tony Curtis, Jon Bon Jovi, this Russian guy and I decided to go up to the Ibiza race track. They got out three of the racing horse and carts for us. Only three because Tony Curtis wasn't up for it, but Bon Jovi jumped straight into one, as did the Russian and I and we had a race around the circuit.

They [racing cars] are terrifying when you're in one and they go a lot faster than you'd think. We were laughing our heads off as we hurtled around – all you can see when you're in one is the horse's arse. For some reason at the end of the day they gave Tony Curtis a big award but he didn't do fuck all!!

I'm not too proud to say that I'm writing this after a little siesta in my room. The allure of a quick lie down in an air-conditioned atmosphere was proving too strong after a selection of strong and delicious drinks. My room gets snippets of intriguing conversations from the back terrace, conspiratorial giggles from the bathrooms, hushed whispers of plans for the night and I'm enjoying people-listening as I prepare to head once more into the breach. The music pumping through the speakers at the pool has had more than a sprinkling of disco and it's getting people into the party spirit (as if they needed much convincing) – you can tell because the singalongs are getting more raucous. I swing my legs over the bed, finish the now melted Margarita I brought along for company, shove on a pair of jeans, sneakers and shirt and open the door. Then, with dazzled eyes, I go back and get my sunglasses. This might sound kind of stupid but as I emerge back into Plaza Mayor, it feels like the hotel's starting to shake its hips to the music. There's a pulse around the hotel and a genuine feeling of excitement. Over the past years, Pikes has quietly been garnering an award-winning reputation for its restaurant, Room 39. Specialising in modern twists on British classics and also using local ingredients as much as possible. With a kitchen nestled within the 500-year-old farmhouse, helmed by Gordon Ramsay alumni Lee Milne, they've been steadily upping the quality of the food for the past five years. "It's the only kitchen I've cooked in that's got walls the width of a flippin' Ford Fiesta" the Welsh chef laughs to me, gesturing to the finca building as we cross paths in Plaza Mayor. "This year we managed to push a hole with a bulldozer through the wall and fit my oven in it. We've got a whole combi oven sitting inside the thickness of the wall." I guess these are the issues you get when you cook in a 500-year-old building.

The day might be heading into evening, but for some people in the hotel, their shift is just beginning, There's a cocktail at Pikes called Captain Of The Night for a reason – it's Mika Jarosz's nickname. When everyone's partying and losing themselves on the dance floor, this man is the night manager and responsible for making sure everything is running smoothly. It takes a special kind of soul to manage the guests at Pikes when the party is in full swing. Like, for instance, when a guest decides to get naked and take a bath in Freddie's during a party, or the time a couple were staying and partying in here. They went back to their room and re-entered the party naked apart from both sporting Russian gas masks. One crawled in on his knees in a dog collar and the other one walked behind him, holding the leash and spanking his boyfriend's bum with a cane... How does a night manager manage this? "Well, I was just walking behind them saying, 'please mind where you are crawling, there is broken glass on the floor, sir!' Mika laughs as we meet in Room 39. He has a few minutes before his earpiece will be crackling with updates all night long so he takes it out, and we grab a stool at the heavy wooden bar while tells me how he ended up at the hotel.

"I was born in Poland to a normal, middle class family," he tells me, "but my mum took the decision to have a better life. So at the end of the Cold War, just before the Berlin Wall came down, we moved as illegals/immigrants to Germany. During that time it was very common in Poland to move away – my family is spread all around the world. I lived in Germany for 22 years before I realised that I must follow the wise ways of my mum and look for my own luck in another country. I gave up my job working in the German music scene and sailed (not literally) to Ibiza. Thanks mum for that, love you forever!"

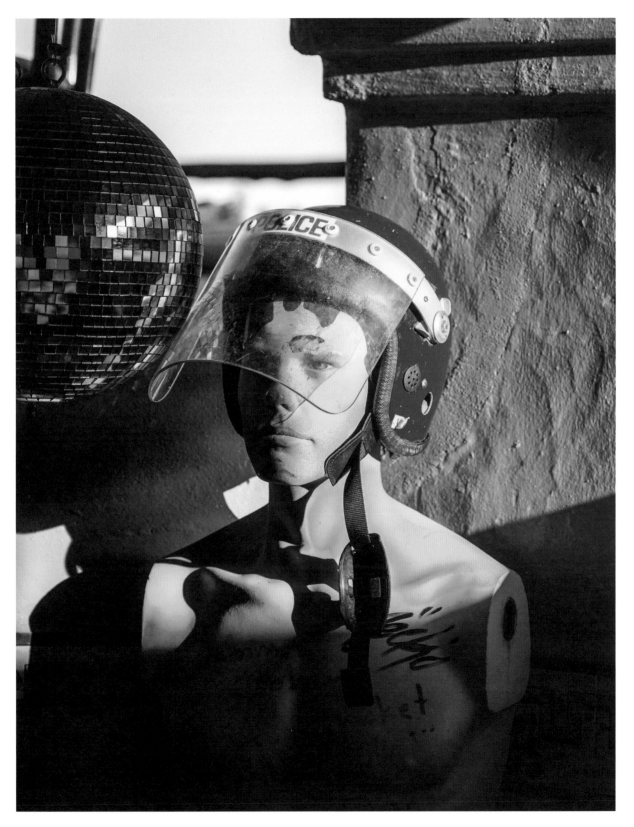

"I arrived in Ibiza feeling like a sailor; just me and one bag. I needed a change, my life felt like it was sticking and freezing in cold Germany. So I decided to take my life on a journey through paradise and chose Ibiza to become my new home. In the early years of this century I spent lot of time on this island having holidays, adventures and always a ball. So I thought, what is the point of leaving? Why don't I just stay here, try and find a job, try and learn a new language, make new friends and live your life in a manner that you choose. It was hard to find a job at first, because I had no clue of the language, but I did have luck on my side and found work as a barman at the famous Ibiza Rocks Hotel – this was the start of all the happiness this island has brought to my life.

I didn't find Pikes, Pikes found me. Stephen Hughes, the Food and Beverage manager here, contacted me and asked if I would be up for an amazing new project working as a barman in a wonderful and hedonistic place. At first I wasn't sure. I had only done two seasons and didn't want to leave my new Ibiza Rocks family. Then Stephen told me that Dawn and Andy would be running this magical place called Pikes. When I heard that, my decision was made. I changed the course of my life and sailed towards new horizons and seas.

Becoming Captain of the Night was the natural evolution and rise from me being a sailor. This is how Pikes works – it's organic. I love it here because it's the best environment to work and develop yourself. This place gives a lot opportunities to be creative, to connect and to meet new people. It's like a big exchange hub full of emotions, happiness, nature, beautiful flowers, birds, blue skies, a stunning pool and lots of other untold secrets. Plus the beautiful clients and colleagues make

this place its own little universe. Our staff really are like a family, we've been working together for seven years now; we have a family vibe and this is the magic that this place creates. The Pikes family will be always a family.

I've had all sorts of things happen to me while I'm working while everyone else is partying. DJ Harvey wearing a kaftan, singing me love songs and dancing the tango, was a highlight, while on Halloween one year, Artwork turned up as a vampire version of myself, the Captain of the Night. Everybody thought he was me – I had an incognito time that night! It was funny to observe it and have a laugh about myself. I have many, many stories, if you want to know more, then come and find me and I will whisper them secretly in your ear...

A witch once read my tarot cards and told me, 'go into your new life, have no fear. You will be living in a yellow house up in the mountains with a sea view.' Perhaps Pikes was always to be my destiny..." and with that, we clink our Dark Horse shots together, down them and Mika plugs in his ear piece and leaves me to start his shift.

I catch the eye of a passing waiter who's ripped the arms off his staff uniform shirt, giving him the air of a late '80s cult film hero. I order a Captain of the Night and on hearing me, Mika turns back and tips his red military hat in a trademark salute.

The Room 39 bar is stocked with seriously high-quality liquor. It has a wider range of drinks than the pool bar. I order a small beer to go with my cocktail and grab the cocktail menu to see what the evening has in store for me. It's definitely going to be a long one. I should pace myself, I think, as I drain both drinks.

MARLEY MARTINI

This is one of the top 10 cocktails requested at our bars. And it's obvious why. It's a cocktail that hits hard in all areas - intense flavours, sweetness, an alcoholic kick and a caffeine rush that'll take you through 'till closing.

Ingredients

Vodka
35 ml/1 1/4 fl.oz.
Kahlúa (or other coffee liqueur)
25 ml/1 fl.oz.
Sugar syrup
10 ml/1/3 fl.oz.
Espresso coffee, cooled
35 ml/1 1/4 fl.oz.
Cubed ice
Garnish: finely ground coffee, coffee beans

Serves 1

How to make

Add cubed ice to a cocktail shaker, then add all of the ingredients and shake well. Double strain into a chilled martini glass. Dust with a little ground coffee and float 3 coffee beans on top to garnish. Serve straightaway.

THE
GLORY HOLE

It's been a while since we filled in the glory hole at Pikes. Many remember the excitement of the idea and the conundrum, a glory hole in a wall that was half a metre thick… Hierbas Ibicencas, bourbon and Campari contribute spirit, and the local protagonists lemon, rosemary and fig add character to the "eyes closed" experience with The Glory Hole that always has a happy ending.

Ingredients

Sweet vermouth
25 ml/1 fl.oz.
Hierbas Ibicencas
25 ml/1 fl.oz.
Woodford Reserve
15 ml/1/2 fl.oz.
Lemon juice
25 ml/1 fl.oz.
Rosemary syrup
15 ml/1/2 fl.oz.
Fig jam
Cubed ice
Garnish: Fresh fig
slices, rosemary sprig

Serves 1

How to make

Add all of the ingredients to a cocktail shaker plus 2 tsps of fig jam. Add cubed ice and shake. Strain into a martini or cocktail glass. Garnish as shown and serve straightaway.

CARELESS WHISPER

Ingredients

Tequila
30 ml/1 fl.oz.
Camomilla (or other
chamomile liqueur)
30 ml/1 fl.oz.
Lime juice
15 ml/1/2 fl.oz.
Pink grapefruit juice
60 ml/2 fl.oz.
Gomme syrup
5 ml/1/6 fl.oz.
Soda water to top up
Cubed and crushed ice
Garnish: Pink
grapefruit slices,
edible flowers

Serves 1

How to make

Add all of the
ingredients apart from
the soda to a cocktail
shaker. Add cubed ice,
shake and strain into
a water glass or
tumbler filled with
crushed ice. Top up
with soda, garnish
as shown and serve
straightaway.

SAME BUT DIFFERENT

Wherever you find yourself, this long and refreshing drink is perfect by day or by night to offer a refreshing respite from the heat and thirst. A simple mix of vodka, Chambord, raspberry and blackberry purée, lemon juice and soda. Served long and strong, you can't go wrong.

Ingredients

Premium vodka
40 ml/1 1/2 fl.oz.
Chambord
20 ml/1/2 fl.oz.
Raspberry and
blackberry purée
15 ml/1/2 fl.oz.
Sugar syrup
10 ml/1/3 fl.oz.
Lemon juice
5 ml/1/6 fl.oz.
Soda water
80-100 ml/3 fl.oz.
Cubed and crushed ice
Garnish: Lemon peel,
blackberries

Serves 1

How to make

Add all of the ingredients (apart from the soda water) to a cocktail shaker. Add cubed ice and shake. Strain into a highball glass filled with crushed ice. Top up with soda water, garnish as shown and serve straightaway.

RON Y SCOTCH

Ingredients

Añejo dark rum
25 ml/1 fl.oz.
Blended Scotch whisky
25 ml/1 fl.oz.
Egg white
20 ml/3/4 fl.oz.
Lime juice
25 ml/1 fl.oz.
Orange juice
10 ml/1/3 fl.oz.
Agave syrup
10 ml/1/3 fl.oz.
Orange bitters
(optional)
Cubed ice

Serves 1

How to make

In a cocktail shaker, dry shake the egg white (i.e. without ice), then add all of the other ingredients apart from the bitters. Add cubed ice and shake hard. Double strain into a chilled coupe glass. Add a few dashes of orange bitters on top of the egg white foam (if desired) and serve straightaway.

HUNG LIKE A MULE

Ingredients

Vodka
30 ml/1 fl.oz.
Elderflower liqueur
20 ml/3/4 fl.oz.
Lime juice
12.5 ml/1/6 fl.oz.
Ginger beer
100 ml/3 1/3 fl.oz.
Small cucumber piece
Cubed ice
Garnish: Lime slices,
mint sprig

Serves 1

How to make

Muddle the cucumber
well in a cocktail
shaker. Add the vodka,
elderflower liqueur and
lime juice. Add cubed
ice, shake hard and
double strain into a
copper tankard filled
with crushed ice. Top
up with ginger beer,
garnish as shown and
serve straightaway.

TONY'S TALES

Ingredients

Dark rum
30 ml/1 fl.oz.
Orange liqueur
20 ml/3/4 fl.oz.
Galliano
15 ml/1/2 fl.oz.
Orange juice
30 ml/1 fl.oz.
Fresh cream
30 ml/1 fl.oz.
Cubed ice

Serves 1

How to make

Add all of the
ingredients to a
cocktail shaker. Add
cubed ice and shake.
Strain into a martini
glass, while recounting
an entrancing story...
and serve straightaway.

HOME OF THE ADULTRESS

This is a love it or hate it cocktail. Its vegetable nature by way of roasted red pepper and chilli has its fans. Mezcal as a base spirit is complex and also has its devotees - particularly of the alcoholic effects, which can leave the consumer high. It's a beautifully balanced cocktail in regards to sweetness, citrus and spice.

Ingredients

Tequila
60 ml/2 fl.oz.
Roasted piquillo pepper
purée
40 ml/2 fl.oz.
Sugar syrup
20 ml/3/4 fl.oz.
Lime juice
15 ml/1/2 fl.oz.
3-5 Cardamom seeds
1 Small red chilli
Cubed ice
Garnish: Dehydrated
lime wheel, small
red chilli

Serves 1

How to make

Muddle the cardamom seeds in a cocktail shaker then add 1/2 the chilli and muddle well. Add the vodka, piquillo pepper purée, sugar syrup and lime juice. Add cubed ice, shake hard and double strain into a chilled martini glass. Garnish as shown and serve straightaway.

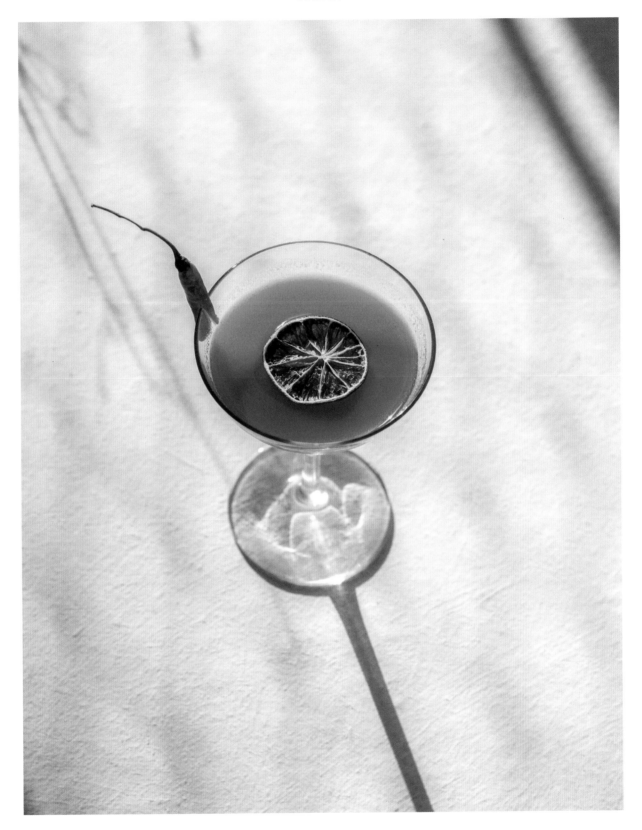

RED
SNAPPER

This smash cocktail is not technical but should be made mindfully. The perfect combination of orange, raspberry and red chilli delivers a mouth-pleasing experience and needs to be balanced dutifully with the sugar and alcohol. The experience is very much the sum of its parts - careful though, as this little number has a big bite.

Ingredients

Premium cachaça
60 ml/2 fl.oz.
Gomme syrup
20 ml/3/4 fl.oz.
5 Fresh raspberries
3 Orange slices
1/2 small red chilli
Cubed and crushed ice
Garnish: Orange slice, raspberries, small red chilli

Serves 1

How to make

Muddle the chilli with the orange slices and raspberries in a cocktail shaker. Add the cachaça and gomme syrup. Add cubed ice and shake well. Strain into a rocks glass filled with crushed ice, garnish as shown and serve straightaway.

VODKA MARTINI

This was one of Tony Pike's preferred cocktails and you'd often see him at the bar sipping one. Saying that, if it wasn't prepared to the strict guidelines of Mr Pikes, then you'd expect a volley of profanity. Very dry, vermouth in and out, dry ice, stirred long but not too long, iced glass and a twist of lemon. A martini purist, we may say, and a legend.

Ingredients

Premium vodka
75 mL/2 1/2 fl.oz.
Dry vermouth
15 mL/1/2 fl.oz
Cubed ice
Garnish: Lemon twist

Serves 1

How to make

Add cubed ice to a mixing glass, such as a Boston shaker glass. Add the vermouth and swirl around the glass and cubed ice, coating everything. Strain out the excess, add the vodka and stir very well (30-45 seconds). Strain into a chilled martini glass, garnish as shown and serve straightaway.

CAIPIRINHA

The Brazilian classic with medicinal roots is still responsible for the comatose state of some. Beware of cachaça - the base liquor has a wicked bite. The danger is that the Caipirinha is simple and surprisingly easy to drink. It's perfectly balanced but loaded with sugar so it catches up on you quickly, knocks you out and can leave you with a memorable hangover.

Ingredients

Premium cachaça
50 ml/1 2/3 fl.oz.
1 Lime cut into eighths
2 level tbsps sugar
Crushed ice
Garnish: Lime wheel

Serves 1

How to make

Muddle the lime wedges with the sugar in a rocks glass, ensuring full extraction of the juice and oils. Add the cachaça and stir well to completely dissolve the sugar. Add crushed ice to half fill the glass, stir well and then top with more crushed ice. Garnish as shown and serve straightaway.

CHAMPAGNE COCKTAIL

Ingredients

Brandy
20 ml/3/4 fl.oz.
Grand Marnier
10 ml/1/3 fl.oz.
1 Sugar cube
Angostura bitters
Champagne to top up
Garnish: Large orange
twist

Serves 1

How to make

First soak the sugar
cube in Angostura
Bitters. Drop the
soaked cube into a
flute, then add the
brandy and the Grand
Marnier. Top up with
chilled Champagne,
garnish as shown and
serve straightaway.

Tony's Tale #4

When anyone famous came to stay, I'd make all the staff go down and welcome them. With Grace Jones, I'd met her at a birthday party in New York through a girl I knew and when she came here I was on a promise…

The taxi pulled up and she got out wearing a matador hat and a cape. She's an incredible person and has this aura about her – she's terrifying. Grace has incredible magnetism, people think she's tall but she's not, she's only about 5' 2". She just swanned up and walked right past me, I didn't even get a chance to say hello. She was in Room 2, so I thought I'd give her a ring.

'That wasn't a very nice welcome,' I said. 'What did you expect? Me to put my arms around you and kiss you? If I did that every magazine in Spain would have that on the front cover,' she replied. I didn't think that was such a bad thing. Then she told me to come down to her room so I hopped in the shower, washed myself squeaky clean, then took myself along to her room and knocked on the door.

We spent several wonderful nights in Room 2, getting to know all about each other. I took her out on a Sunseeker boat and we had a bottle of champagne and both took a pill. It hit us straight away. I was looking at her and said, 'Right now, you're not Grace Jones, you're Elizabeth.' Her full name is Grace Elizabeth Jones. 'Elizabeth Jones is a different person to Grace Jones,' she said. 'You're one of the first men in my life that's picked that up so quickly.'

I could see her aura – it wasn't the drugs, it was just the moment. I put my hand through this incredible aura and touched her face. It was amazing. 'How?' I said. 'Love?' she replied. 'Do you think that you're falling in love?' I said. 'Maybe – it's possible,' she said, before adding, 'Do you want to make love now?'

I really did.

It's now been an hour or two since dinner and I'm feeling glorious – I've got two empty Martini glasses in front of me and am hankering to empty a third, but everyone knows three Martinis spell trouble later on. I'm enjoying the warm buzz that the other two left me with and have moved to a table that overlooks the pool. We're past dusk now and I've been watching the newly scrubbed up guests emerging from their rooms and heading either to the bar or to reception to catch a taxi some place. Bugs whirr past me on their way to dance around the night lights that have come on across the hotel.

I finally spy the man I've been wanting to sit down with – Stephen Hughes. I thought that as I'm writing this cocktail book I should really have a drink with the man who designed the whole 66-cocktail menu. Steve, like virtually everyone on the Pikes staff, had a rich and colourful history before finding himself working at the hotel. He's a beautiful soul, with a sharp sartorial style and, with the tiniest motions of his hand, makes sure the bar staff bring me a medley of cocktails as he tells his Pikes story.

'I've been in Food and Beverage for years and I've worked around the world in bars and restaurants. In 1999 I was back in the UK working in London with Antony Worrall Thompson in one of the first organic restaurants. I came to Ibiza for a holiday that year and when I went back he had decided to close it. I took redundancy and the opportunity to travel again. I left London, first going back to Ibiza, and decided to take a break from F&B. Over the next few years I floated between Ibiza and Bahia, Brazil. In the winter of 2005, I bumped in the owner of El Ayoun, the bar/restaurant in Ibiza's San Rafael. He asked me to come and work with them the next summer and

although I'd been out of restaurants for years I was thinking I wouldn't mind a more secure job for a change. I went to work in the bar, cocktail bartending again and El Ayoun was a very good bar at a good time; 2006 was the peak year of that place.

I worked in a few other places in Ibiza then, in the winter of 2011, met Andy and Dawn. I was actually doing some building work at their house and got chatting to Dawn. I told her about my life in bars and restaurants and she asked if I fancied going to Pikes with them. It sounded quite good but I'd never been to Pikes, so I didn't really know what to expect.

When we came up to Pikes it was night and all the lights were on. I walked up the path thinking, "Wow, this place is nice. It's like a special place where special things happen." That proved to be right in more ways than one as I met my life partner here that year. Pikes was quite rundown at that time, a lot of the operation was broken or didn't function. We went to the bar at the bottom of the road for a drink and Mike Bayon, the Ibiza Rocks Travel Director at that time, said over a *caña*, "OK Steve you're gonna be the Food and Beverage Manager".

When I walked around that first day I looked at the pool bar and it soon became apparent that I would need to make a few changes to the layout. The bar was something that had evolved over the last 20 years and was designed to serve no more than a handful of guests. I was a bricklayer, so remodelling the inside of the bar to make it more functional and creating at least one work station was a relatively small task. Having this construction insight means I can understand what a gargantuan task building Pikes was over the years, and it reinforced the respect I have for Tony and his vision.

That year, the occupancy of Pikes for the summer was virtually zero; there was a restaurant but it was empty. Whenever I was out around Ibiza and spoke to people about Pikes it was always "I love Pikes, amazing place" but if you asked them the last time they'd been here it was nearly always "oh, years ago". We finally opened after weeks of immense effort, getting everything functioning again and putting up the truckloads of curiosities and decorations that Dawn had started to ferry in from her shopping escapades. The beginning was very, very slow. I remember the first chef, Sam, imagining that we were going open and it was going to be full of people immediately. But the reality of opening a restaurant in Ibiza is not like London. What happens is the first year could be dead, and a successful second year might have 10 or 20% more people coming in. I take my hat off to Andy and Dawn. Pikes was a complicated place to take on, you needed the vision and determination to nail it. They nailed it and are still nailing it!

By the end of year two, people started coming here again, saying how magical the place was. It was as if you could feel the magic of what was to come just hanging in the air, all it needed was the people. Although the project was exciting, you had to be prepared for the reality – it was going to be a long game, word of mouth would be what put us back on the map and the rise would take some years. Real characters are never in short supply here and the open atmosphere allows people to engage and make lasting friendships really easily. I think the key is that nobody takes themselves that seriously. In 2017 we became more commercial, but it happened by default. I felt a shift happen, like we'd moved up a gear. It was inevitable and we are still very careful how we manage this success. We are always striving to maintain the authenticity

and we know the people that you find at Pikes are the key to that as much as is holding onto and respecting the history here. When people congratulate us for bringing Pikes back to what it is today I share that compliment with them. I genuinely believe above all, the friends of Pikes are what has contributed to this success, the juxtaposition of the team, the guest, Pikes and Ibiza is the magic that you feel.´ On realising that he has to run to a meeting (there's never any rest for a Food and Beverage Manager), Steve orders me a Sexy Priest – the first time anybody's ever done that for me.

"TIME FOR SHOTS." Uh oh... I recognise that voice. A tall, striking lady with a distinctive eastern European accent playfully cuffs me on the head as she slides into a chair across the table with a fully loaded tray. The selection of four shots that now sit between me and my new companion mean that my evening is 100% about to level up. I'm facing staff member Lucie Rekosava, who found her way to Pikes from her native Czech Republic via China, Singapore and accidentally auditioning to be a Playboy Bunny at the Ibiza Rocks Hotel. The Bunny life wasn't what kept her on the island though. It was the sense of being at home when she moved up the hill to Pikes, working on the door at first and then working on the events. "There really is a sense of family at this company – a slightly dysfunctional one." she says as we down the first of the four shots. "Somehow I ended up on the door at Pikes doing the guest list, and I just fell in love with the place. Somehow, after feeling like an outsider for a majority of my life, I finally felt like I belonged and I've not left since."

"SHOTS FOR EVERYONE" she announces, and heads to the bar where I can see the staff laughing and shaking their heads.

HIERBAS IBICENCAS

On a trip to Ibiza it's unlikely that you won't come across Hierbas. Many regions of Spain have their signature liqueur, and this is the signature of Ibiza and the mainstay of the local Ibicencan bar scene. A liqueur infused with a selection of local aromatic herbs, its familiar flavour is the taste of Ibiza for many tourists. A shot of Hierbas is a common end to a meal or toast on a night out. Don't be surprised to find a shot in your hand after the cry of "shots for everyone!" is heard ringing around Pikes. We're looking at you Lucie…

Ingredients

Hierbas Ibicencas
(herbal liqueur
from Ibiza)
30 ml/1 fl.oz.

Serves 1

How to make

Fill shot glasses with the Hierbas Ibicencas liqueur, then empty the shots in one quick drink. Easy!

HONEY DIJON

There's something comforting about the colour orange; it's as soothing as this cocktail. Gin is the spirit base, limoncello adds some weight and a citric depth, honey adds warmth. The real protagonist of this cocktail, though, has to be the carrot juice. We firmly believe you should take any opportunity to get fresh juice into yourself and what better way than through a delicious cocktail?

Ingredients

Gin
30 ml/1 fl.oz.
Limoncello
20 ml/1 fl.oz.
Carrot juice
80 ml/2 3/4 fl.oz.
Lemon juice
15 ml/1/2 fl.oz.
Liquid honey
5 ml/1/6 fl.oz.
Orange bitters
Cubed ice
Garnish: Thyme sprig

Serves 1

How to make

Add all of the ingredients to a cocktail shaker with a few dashes of orange bitters. Add cubed ice, then shake and strain into a martini glass. Garnish as shown and serve straightaway.

STIRRED NOT SHAKEN

Ingredients

Premium bourbon
60 mL/2 fl.oz.
Ginger ale or beer
(depending on the
level of heat you
like), to top up
2 Lime quarters
Cubed ice

Serves 1

How to make

Build the bourbon and
ginger ale (or beer)
in a highball glass
over cubed ice. Squeeze
the juice from the lime
wedges over the top and
then drop the wedges
into the glass and
serve straightaway.

ALL THAT JAZZ

When Ronnie Scott's are visiting us it really is all about that jazz. This vodka-based cocktail is fresh, fruity - the Cava delivers a lovely effervescence at the end and the mild mint tones bring a clean finish to the experience. What better way to enjoy the music than to sit at your table sipping one of these cocktails.

Ingredients

Premium vodka
35 ml/1 1/4 fl.oz.
Grapefruit juice
30 ml/1 fl.oz.
Mango syrup
25 ml/1 fl.oz.
Chilli syrup
15 ml/1/2 fl.oz.
5-6 Mint leaves
Cava to top up
Cubed ice
Garnish: Grapefruit twist

Serves 1

How to make

Muddle the mint leaves in a cocktail shaker. Add the vodka, grapefruit juice and both the syrups. Add cubed ice and shake well. Double strain into a coupe glass and top up with chilled cava. Garnish as shown and serve straightaway.

THE
DARK HORSE

A cocktail for the ladies – but don't be fooled by this little number. It really does have a kick, hence its name. Lime juice, forest fruits and mint smashed together give this a fruity-citrus base, and the cachaça adds the kick.

Ingredients	How to make
Premium cachaça 60 ml/2 fl.oz. Fruits of the forest (berry) purée 30 ml/1 fl.oz. Sugar syrup 25 ml/1 fl.oz. 1/4 Lime Crushed ice Garnish: Lime slice, blackberry, mint leaf	Muddle the lime quarter at the bottom of a small rocks glass to extract the juice and citrus oils. Add the fruits of the forest purée, sugar syrup and cachaça. Stir well, top with crushed ice and stir again. Garnish as shown and serve straightaway.

Serves 1

IN LOVE
AT LAST

The complex properties of mezcal marry beautifully
with the lush, over ripe grapes of sauternes.
The sweetness of the dessert wine transports the
delicate fruit to the front line of this cocktail
where it complements the astringent character of
the mezcal. Grapefruit bitters add an extra depth
and the egg white gives a creamy texture.

Ingredients

Mezcal joven
30 ml/1 fl.oz.
Sauternes sweet wine
40 ml/1 1/2 fl.oz.
Pink grapefruit juice
50 ml/1 2/3 fl.oz.
Agave syrup
5 ml/1/6 fl.oz.
Egg white
20 ml/ 3/4 fl.oz.
Grapefruit bitters
Cubed ice
Garnish: Grapefruit
twist

How to make

Dry shake the egg
white in a cocktail
shaker (i.e. without
ice), then add all of
the ingredients apart
from the bitters. Add
cubed ice, shake hard
and double strain
into a chilled coupe
glass. Add 2 dashes of
grapefruit bitters on
top of the egg white
foam, garnish as shown
and serve straightaway.

#note: For best
results, choose an
unaged mezcal joven for
its smooth flavour.

OLD FASHIONED

Ingredients

Premium bourbon
60 ml/2 fl.oz.
Maraschino syrup
5 ml/1 tsp
Orange peel strip
Sugar cube
Angostura bitters
1/2 tsp water
Cubed ice
Garnish: Orange zest,
Maraschino cherry

Serves 1

How to make

Muddle the orange peel
strip in a rocks glass
with the Maraschino
syrup, sugar cube,
2 dashes of Angostura
bitters and water.
When the sugar has
dissolved, add the
bourbon and stir until
well mixed. Add cubed
ice and stir well.
Garnish as shown and
serve straightaway.

THE BIG LICK

The perfect way to deliver a shot of tequila. The Mangita chaser cools down the spirit and leaves a fruity, herbaceous mouth feel. Based on the concept of Sangrita or Verdita, the traditional Mexican chaser, at Pikes we favour mango and grapefruit as our base. And the salt and chilli dusted on the side of the shot glass is for those who are up for the big lick…

Ingredients

Tequila
30 ml/1 fl.oz.
Pikes Mangita
(see #note)
30 ml/1 fl.oz.
Garnish: Salt and
chilli flakes to dust
the side of the glass

Serves 1

How to make

Pour the tequila into a shot glass and set aside. Moisten the side of a second shot glass with water and dust the sides of it with the salt and chilli flakes. Fill the dusted glass with chilled Pikes Mangita. Drink the tequila first, then the mangita.

#note: To make Pikes Mangita, prepare the quantity you need based on a single-serving blend of 30 ml/1 fl.oz. grapefruit juice, 25 ml/1 fl.oz. mango purée, 20 ml/3/4 fl.oz sugar syrup and a sprig of fresh coriander/cilantro plus a few mint leaves. Fine strain and seal and it will keep in the fridge for up to 5 days.

THE SEXY PRIEST

Dawn's inspiration for the Potting Shed bar was to create a drinking shrine that would be a second home to all types. A place where your grandad would feel as at home as a hot Italian priest. The Sexy Priest cocktail on the contrary has one divine focus: apple. Calvados, green apple syrup and freshly squeezed cloudy apple juice combine to offer one hell of a holy experience. Bless you.

Ingredients

Calvados
50 ml/1 2/3 fl.oz.
Green apple syrup
25 ml/1 fl.oz.
Clear apple juice
75 ml/2 1/2 fl.oz.
Cubed ice
Garnish: Green apple fan

Serves 1

How to make

Add all of the ingredients to a cocktail shaker and add cubed ice. Shake and strain into a rocks glass filled with fresh cubed ice. Garnish as shown and serve straightaway.

CRYSTAL DILDO

The Crystal Dildo has been a big seller at Room 39, the name alone is most certainly attention grabbing... It's fruity and on the sweet side, but the blood orange syrup helps to soften the aged mezcal and allows the pleasant and memorable delivery of this most mystical of spirits.

Ingredients

Mezcal reposado
(see #note)
50 ml/1 2/3 fl.oz.
Orange juice
30 ml/1 fl.oz.
Blood orange syrup
15 ml/1/2 fl.oz.
Cacao syrup
15 ml/1/2 fl.oz.
Cubed ice

Serves 1

How to make

Build all of the ingredients in a cocktail shaker and add cubed ice. Shake hard, double strain into a chilled coupe glass and serve straightaway.

#note: For best results, use an oak-aged mezcal reposado for a fuller flavour.

Tony's Tale #5

I was doing some painting one day and a stunning English woman walked up to reception. She was gorgeous so I went down to introduce myself. She was the American beauty Koo Stark and she said the hotel was exactly what she was looking for, as the paparazzi were on her tail because of those stories about her and a certain English prince. I took her to Room 11 and went to the bar to get a bucket of ice and bottle of champagne...

As I was heading back, a Rolls Royce came to a stop just outside and two guys in black suits got out. They said they'd been instructed to check the place out by their boss and they liked what they saw. They wouldn't divulge who their boss was, but they wanted to take eight rooms for three weeks, gave me $3,000 cash as a deposit and said he would be flying in the next day.

That weekend Pikes was in a *Sunday Express* story saying there was cocaine on the breakfast menu... The police chief hated me and made me go down to his office on Monday morning, where I had to explain to him that it was a load of rubbish but he still said that he was going to keep his eye on me.

That was a bad start to the week, but then this mysterious boss arrived and it happened to be Julio Iglesias.

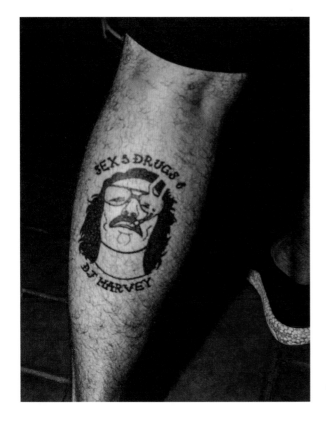

I try to work out how much I've had to drink since I arrived. This morning seems like days ago and those shots seem to have broken my maths, so I give up. I decide to take a stroll to the other side of Plaza Mayor, nipping down through a low stone passageway that has a fantastic neon sign opposite Sunny's Boudoir that asks "Why The Fuck Can't I Have Fun All The Time?" and leads out onto the back terrace.

It's buzzing out here - there are seven or eight antique double beds, which are smothered in party goers, leather banquettes, chairs and tables, a cocktail bar in a shed and a bigger bar further up. Maybe it's the shirts and dresses but things appear to have just grown up, just a little bit, on this side of the hotel. People have swapped the bucket goblets of gin and tonic and tall, creamy Punka Coladas for delicate drinks in delicate glasses. Maybe it's to reflect their outfit changes, maybe the evenings are more cultured after midnight.

I see a photographer friend of mine lounging on a leather banquette. He tells me it's the same one he shot Irvine Welsh and Carl Barât on during the Pikes Literary Festival - he ended up having a back-to-my-room party with them after hours, where they decided the name of his newborn baby. Of course he did. I wonder to him if he'll ever tell his kid that story. Right now he's not sure if he even wants to tell his wife that's how he came up with it.

A group of beautiful people dripping in glad rags are sitting on one of the beds and they all erupt into gales of laughter as though someone's just said something they really shouldn't have. As I look over I recognise one of them and know it's almost certain he's the source of the group eruption.

It's Pike's own VIP host and guest relations, the indomitable Sunny Ramzan. He seems to be wearing some kind of firefighters hood. Or maybe he's nicked one of the Starlight Express hat things that are scattered around the pool. I can't really tell. Whatever it is, he's obviously enjoying himself.

Sunny has become part of Pikes lore and visitors are genuinely disappointed if they happen to miss him during one of their stays. Originally starting as a receptionist and host for the Ibiza Rocks parties, he knows every nook and cranny of the place - and has an encyclopaedic knowledge of faces of guests past and present. With a just-vague-enough job title, Sunny's now infamous for hosting the karaoke jacuzzi ball pool room on the right-hand side as you walk into Freddie's, being everybody's friend, and also inviting select people into his very own boudoir - a dressing-up cornucopia that only he has a key to. Whatever happens in Sunny's boudoir definitely stays there.

I watch him expertly prise himself away from the group and head to the bar to recharge his glass. I give him a whistle and beckon him over. Things haven't quite kicked off to peak busy yet so with a wink and a wave he sidles down the terrace and perches on a wall next to me. For someone with an international reputation for being a lot of whole lot of fun, Sunny's actually fairly quietly spoken.

He has known and worked with Dawn and Andy from their Manumission days and now has a role cemented at the very core of the Pikes experience. Learning from the master of hosts Tony Pike, Sunny can be found flitting around the pool during the day with time to talk to everyone, At night he really comes into his own, hosting the aforementioned frivolity as

the sun sets and later on into the night. But it wasn't always singing in ball pools and dressing up he tells me over an Adult Kindergarten, delicately holding the stem and peering at me over the flower-filled glass with a perfectly arched eyebrow.

"I was doing karaoke in Chez Fez in a nightclub; with a mic stand, and on a stage, and it worked... on occasions. But it was a tricky one to sell. It was actually my dream but because I was told to do it, my heart wasn't in it – it felt false. It was just an empty gap that they wanted me to fill in. If I'd been allowed the creative freedom, I would have smashed it.

Anyway, we did a few of those, and then, while the season was in full swing, and we were preparing to do the Freddie Mercury night in 2013, Leanne, who was our events manager back then, came up with a genius idea. She said, 'Sunny, how do you feel about taking the karaoke into the jacuzzi in Freddie's?' Who would have thought? Not in a million years! She just thought, we've got an empty bathtub so let's put some balls in there. So I said, 'Alright, drop me in that bathtub and I'll give it a whirl!'

From the first minute, I knew we were on to a winner. Back then we actually had a few kids at the event while it was still early, like 10pm. There was this one lad who had came dressed as Freddie Mercury – I mean he was literally 10 years old, but he wanted to sing. His parents were there, and I thought, well, brilliant, OK then. He got in the bath, and when I asked him what he wanted to sing, he goes, 'Have you got Blurred Lines by Robin Thicke?' I'm like, erm what? So that was one of the first tracks we did in the bathtub. It was a ten-year-old, dressed as Freddie Mercury, singing Blurred Lines. So that's how bathtub karaoke started. The room where my boudoir is

now... well, that used to be a gift shop/boutique, where you could go and you know, buy fancy goods. That winter when it was empty I jokingly said to Dawn, how do you feel if I turn that into my dressing-up room? She thought it was a brilliant idea, but then she had to go to the moneymen and explain it to them, that 'Sunny needs that room.' I was like, she's only gone and done it!

I've never been keen on the word hedonistic. From my side, I've never felt that was the direction I hoped Pikes would go in and I don't think it really is. It's flamboyant, it's decadent, it's sensational. With hedonism there's no respect; there's no self-respect. I know coming from me it sounds a little... but I have to be aware of my surroundings. Of course I encourage a little bit of extravagance and excess, but with style, with panache. And because Pikes is such an intimate space, I think everyone needs to really respect each other. I prefer to use the word escapism. I know there are moments at Pikes that are electric. When the components that make an evening all come together and people go away with an experience that they'll never forget, that's when we've finally hit the nail on the head. People want to escape from their lives and I'm there to provide that. I'm there to bring people out of their shells."

And with that Sunny sets off to find shells to get people out of. He pushes himself off the wall and heads off down the steps towards his boudoir, sequinned kaftan flapping behind him as guests high five, hug and take selfies with him. I can't think of another hotel in the world where such staff exist. I think it's because none of it is forced, this is exactly what everyone is like, they're not having to play a character. It's a mad place.

LEAP OF FAITH

Ingredients

Vodka
60 ml/2 fl.oz.
Premium dry vermouth
5 ml/1/6 fl.oz.
Cranberry liqueur
10 ml/1/3 fl.oz.
Cubed ice
Garnish: Lemon twist

Serves 1

How to make

Build all of the
ingredients in a Boston
shaker glass and add
cubed ice. Cover with
the shaker and shake
hard. Double strain
into a chilled cocktail
glass. Garnish as shown
and serve straightaway.

VESPER MARTINI

Ingredients

Premium gin
60 ml/2 fl.oz.
Premium vodka
20 ml/3/4 fl.oz.
Lillet blanc
10 ml/1/3 fl.oz.
Cubed ice
Garnish: Lemon twist

Serves 1

How to make

Add all of the
ingredients to a Boston
shaker glass filled
with cubed ice. Cover
with the shaker, shake
well and double strain
into a chilled martini
glass. Garnish as shown
and serve straightaway.

ORIGINAL LOST BOY

Ingredients

Vodka
50 ml/1 2/3 fl.oz.
Lemon juice
15 ml/1/2 fl.oz.
Sugar syrup
15 ml/1/2 fl.oz.
Fig jam
20 ml/3/4 fl.oz.
5 Fresh raspberries
Lemon bitters
Cubed ice
Garnish: Fig slice,
fresh raspberries

Serves 1

How to make

Muddle the raspberries
in a cocktail shaker,
then add the remaining
ingredients along
with 2 dashes of lemon
bitters. Add cubed
ice and shake hard.
Double strain into a
small rocks glass filled
with fresh cubed ice.
Garnish as shown and
serve straightaway.

SUNNY'S GAY G&T

It's suspected that this cocktail has magical powers. At Pikes we believe that it's the secret to the longevity of Sunny's party marathons. A classic G&T with a twist of orange, a stick of cinnamon and few frozen forest fruits to accentuate the hue and there you have it, pink, proud and party power.

Ingredients

Premium gin
50 ml/1 2/3 fl.oz.
Quality tonic water
Cubed ice
Garnish: Orange zest,
frozen fruits of the
forest (berries),
cinnamon stick

Serves 1

How to make

Fill a large balloon glass (ideally a Spanish G&T copa) with cubed ice. Add the gin and top up with chilled tonic water. Twist the orange zest to release its oils before dropping it into the glass. Add the frozen berries and cinnamon stick and serve straightaway.

CROWNING GLORY

Ingredients

Kraken black spiced rum
250 ml/8 1/2 fl.oz.
Passion fruit juice
150 ml/5 fl.oz.
Lime juice
50 ml/1 2/3 fl.oz.
Pineapple juice
1 l/34 fl.oz.
Hazelnut syrup
100 ml/3 1/3 fl.oz.
Chocolate bitters
Cubed ice
Garnish: Grated nutmeg,
caramelized pineapple
wedges, passion fruit,
foraged flora

Serves 4–5

How to make

Build all of the
ingredients over
2 cocktail shakers,
adding a dash of
chocolate bitters
to each. Add cubed ice,
shake well and strain
into a punch bowl
filled with fresh cubed
ice. Top up the ice,
grate over some nutmeg
and garnish as shown.
Serve straightaway with
long paper straws so
everyone can share.

PAPILLON PLAYBOY

The butterflies tattooed on Tony Pike's chest were a testament to how close to his heart his favourite book Papillon was. Tony's playboy image always preceded him and he was always a hit with the ladies. So because of that, the Papillon Playboy is perfectly balanced, a hit with the ladies and gents at Pikes and a cocktail experience that many hold close to their heart.

Ingredients

Butter-washed Vodka
(see #note)
50 ml/1 2/3 fl.oz.
Yuzu juice
25 ml/1 fl.oz.
Vanilla syrup
25 ml/1 fl.oz.
Egg white
20 ml/3/4 fl.oz.
Peychaud's bitters
Cubed ice

Serves 1

How to make

Dry shake the egg white in a cocktail shaker then add all other ingredients, apart from the bitters. Add cubed ice, shake hard and double strain into a coupe glass. Add a few drops of Peychaud's bitters on top of the egg foam and serve straightaway.

#note: To make Butter-washed Vodka, melt 125 g/9 tbsps butter. Combine with 375 ml/ 13 fl. oz. vodka. Stir, seal and leave to sit at room temperature for 3 hours. Transfer to the fridge for 2 hours, until the butter has solidified. Scoop off the layer of butter and pass the vodka through a fine-mesh strainer. Store in a bottle in the fridge for up to 1 week.

CAPTAIN OF THE NIGHT

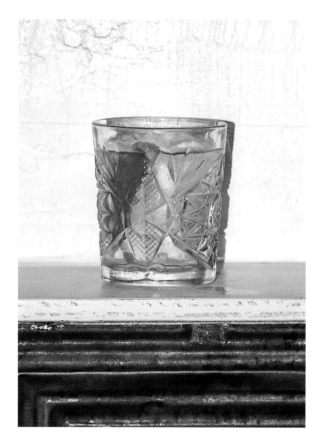

Ingredients

Mezcal reposado
(see #note)
50 ml/1 2/3 fl.oz.
Dry sherry
20 ml/3/4 fl.oz.
Tobacco syrup
10 ml/1/3 fl.oz.
Grapefruit bitters
Cubed ice
Garnish: Grapefruit
slice or zest

Serves 1

How to make

Add all of the
ingredients to an
ice-filled mixing glass
or glass from a Boston
shaker. Add 3 dashes
of grapefruit bitters,
stir for just 30
seconds. Strain over
fresh cubed ice in a
rocks glass. Garnish
as shown and serve
straightaway.

#note: For the best
results use an oak-aged
'reposado' mezcal here
for a fuller flavour.

ADULT KINDERGARTEN

Ingredients

Gin
40 ml/1 1/2 fl.oz.
Red grapefruit juice
20 ml/3/4 fl.oz.
Violet syrup
10 ml/1/3 fl.oz.
Rose syrup
10 ml/1/3 fl.oz.
Cava
100 ml/3 1/3 fl.oz.
Grapefruit bitters
Cubed ice
Soda water to top up
Garnish: Edible flowers

Serves 1

How to make

Add the gin, grapefruit juice, violet and rose syrups plus a dash of grapefruit bitters to a cocktail shaker. Add cubed ice, shake and strain into a large wine glass filled with cubed ice. Add the chilled cava and top with with soda water. Garnish as shown and serve straightaway.

PRIMA BALLERINA

On the wall in Room 39, in among all the curiosities, you'll find a painting of a smiling ballerina, curtsying. Who she is, we have no idea, but it's the perfect introduction to this cocktail. The freshness of this drink is notable and presses all the buttons. Creamy, fruity, minty with a mild effervescence. The Prima Ballerina leaves a lasting impression – maybe order two… two of them.

Ingredients

Apple vodka
50 ml/1 2/3 fl.oz.
Lime juice
20 ml/3/4 fl.oz.
Peach syrup
10 ml/1/3 fl.oz.
Sugar syrup
20 ml/3/4 fl.oz.
Egg white
Soda water to top up
5-6 Mint leaves
Cubed ice
Garnish: Dehydrated green apple slice, ground cinnamon

Serves 1

How to make

Dry shake the egg white in a cocktail shaker (i.e. without ice) and then add all the ingredients apart from the soda. Add cubed ice, shake hard and double strain over fresh cubed ice in a rocks glass. Top up with chilled soda, garnish as shown and serve straightaway.

Tony's Tale #6

I was working on the hotel, like I always am at the beginning of all my stories, and a guy came up asking to speak to the boss. He didn't believe it was me at first but then we introduced ourselves. He said;
"My name's Freddie Mercury."
"My name's Anthony Pike."
"I think we should be friends."
"I think we already are…"

Freddie's 41st birthday was amazing. He used to call me in my room all the time to 'discuss things'. This one time he said his birthday was coming up and could I give him the best private party the island had ever seen. "Freddie, for you I can do practically anything."
"I want to do it with Elton John, we've got similar birthdays and can split the cost between us."
"Do you really want to do that?"
"Well, he's a good friend; I think it would be wonderful."

At the time John Reid was Elton's manager and Jim Beach was Freddie's and there was animosity between the two, so the joint party didn't end up happening.

John's one of only three people I've thrown out of Pikes since it opened. Another said he was the pilot for the Queen of England. He was sprawled across the bar and I threw him out for swearing too much. The third was the managing director of an airline. His friends kept running and pissing in the hotel room bathrooms and when I asked them to stop, this Irish guy offered to fight me, calling me a coward – he had a bodyguard with him. I had to ask them to leave.

As they went, Prince Ernst August of Hanover arrived to stay for his honeymoon. The Prince came up to me and said, "That man leaving said he was going to come back and "kill the Australian bastard". He meant me. I had a friend who was a Scottish wrestler so I rang him and he came up with his lads. As I had Prince Ernst here I couldn't afford a brawl. Luckily, the Irish guy didn't come back so it just ended with me, a Scottish wrestler and Prince Ernst having a drink and a laugh about it.

After Midnight

Things are getting a bit blurrrry – I'm sitting with a film director from Sunderland who works in high fashion and he's been educating me on how to prepare for farming post-apocalypse. He seems to know his stuff and the secret to our survival lies in Bali, I think - it was kind of a hard conversation to follow.

By now the focus of the hotel is squarely on Freddie's, the 300ish capacity nightclub named after the infamous Queen frontman because it was originally the suite that he'd stay in when he visited.

It's a tongue-in-cheek posthumous tribute, as Tony Pike would often like to recount to the people gathered around him at the pool. "When Freddie Mercury stayed at the hotel I put him in the Julio Suite and he called me up and asked me 'Why's this called the Julio Suite?' I said, 'Well Freddie, it's named after a famous international singer. If you keep singing, Freddie, I'm not promising anything – I'll name a tool shed after you...' I was taking the piss you see. He called me a bastard."

When the wind's right it really is as if it's blowing the echoes of Tony's stories around the place - especially the infamous tale about when Freddie held his outrageous 41st birthday party at the hotel.

Since chatting with Sunny, I've had some shots with an Irish designer, had a boisterous room party with some lads from South East London, and met the wonderful drag queen, Ruby Murry in Sunny's boudoir. I could tell you what happened in there but that really is against the rules. Aside from her wonderful company and repartee, Ruby is the fat lady that sings at the end of every Saturday night party to signify that it's finally over. She belts out

Nessun Dorma and has been part of the Pikes family since 2015. Fatboy Slim is also a regular to the hotel - in fact one of his most memorable moments there was the start of a famous relationship. "Towards the end of a spectacular night I took a Radio 1 DJ who I had just met back there just to shower and freshen up before doing her breakfast show (she didn't actually sleep there). There must have been some magic in the air because I ended up marrying her... I have stayed so many times it is like a second home to me. One summer I lived there long enough to get to know all the staff and I almost explored every nook and cranny (it is impossible to know them all!) DJ Harvey makes the place his own, he transports you back to a bygone time of love and hedonism that we could previously only imagine... My birthday in 2019 was a real high - the crowd sang 'Happy Birthday' to me before I had played a single note. Surrounded by friends old and new and my family we all went on a sweaty odyssey that ended with me playing 'Everyone's a Winner' by Hot Chocolate."

All roads lead to Freddie's once the clock passes midnight at Pikes - people drift towards it. Maybe it's a natural magnet or maybe it's because everyone really wants to party hard. Especially tonight as it's DJ Harvey and his world famous Mercury Rising residency. As Swedish superstar Robyn says, "Ibiza opened me up to a new way of relating to music and spending quality time with my friends. When I discovered Pikes, it gave me another dimension to going to the island that I was longing for but had never experienced there before, except for at house parties. Something more intimate and relaxed. The atmosphere that they have nurtured from Tony Pike says a lot about what kind of place it is. It's about things like the free door, the mix of people and DJ Harvey's summer residency. I've had some of my most magical

dance evenings at Freddie's, listening to DJ Harvey there."
I make my way into Freddie's via the back entrance. The Potting Shed is an anteroom found through a hidden bookshelf in Freddie's that in turn leads to the back terrace. It's dark and murky with all kinds of nooks and crannies to hide in. It has a tiny bar surrounded with framed pictures of good-looking priests and is famously where Mr Mercury first performed the song Barcelona before heading to the Ku Club to debut it in front of TV cameras. As Tony remembers it, "Freddie Mercury singing that song in that small room was so powerful. We left here and went up to Ku Club – Freddie had got into his dinner suit and bow tie. There were ten cameras on tracks to get every angle. When the song finished all the cameramen were crying. It was amazing. I was up in the VIP with a girl and found I was holding this girl's hand. I introduced myself and apologised for grabbing her hand, that I'd just got carried away. We went back to her house, she cooked me dinner and we took a bottle of champagne and looked out at the sea – one thing led to another. It was a magic time."

The bass from the main room throbs and pulls me further into the club. It's amazing that this many people can fit into what was an old bedroom suite. Red and green lights bounce off the giant poker chips and rustic crucifixes that adorn the white walls. Funnily enough for a late-night party in Ibiza, everybody is smiling and hugging one another... Of course they are. An enormous disco ball dangles above the intimate crowd reflecting the laser lights in untold directions. It's sweaty and closely packed, bodies bump and grind and arms are aloft while DJ Harvey preaches at

them with his records from the raised DJ booth in the corner. I'm beginning to think there might have been a bit more than gin and tonic in the drinks I had back with the South London lads – I thought the brackish taste was down to the mixer. Maybe I shouldn't have had three of them. I fight the overwhelming urge to stroke the ponytail of the guy in front of me and concentrate on the music. It gets deep into my bones, guiding my body's movements.

Harvey is much more than a DJ who just comes to Pikes for a summer residency. As his infamous Mercury Rising nights have evolved over five years at the hotel he's got more involved in the place. So much so that he's now, officially, the hotel's Cultural Attaché. He was heavily instrumental in the redesign of the sound system and lighting rig in the nightclub. He even goes so far to fill the place up with lilies to stimulate the sense of smell, along with the sight and sound of his set. "Oi!" he shouts to a party goer who's reaching skywards, dipping the volume for a second. "Don't fuck with the disco ball." He means it - Harvey is really serious about the disco ball. Such are his preparations for each show he even controls how fast that ball rotates and doesn't want anyone messing it up. I'm pretty sure that's the only rule of the night though. The crowd nod and laugh and the night carries on. Mika walks past and high fives me on his rounds, keeping things just about in order. The crowd's moving as one and there's a communal, almost spiritual feeling of joy. This is Ibiza, this is the original vibe. Pure freedom. Pure enjoyment.

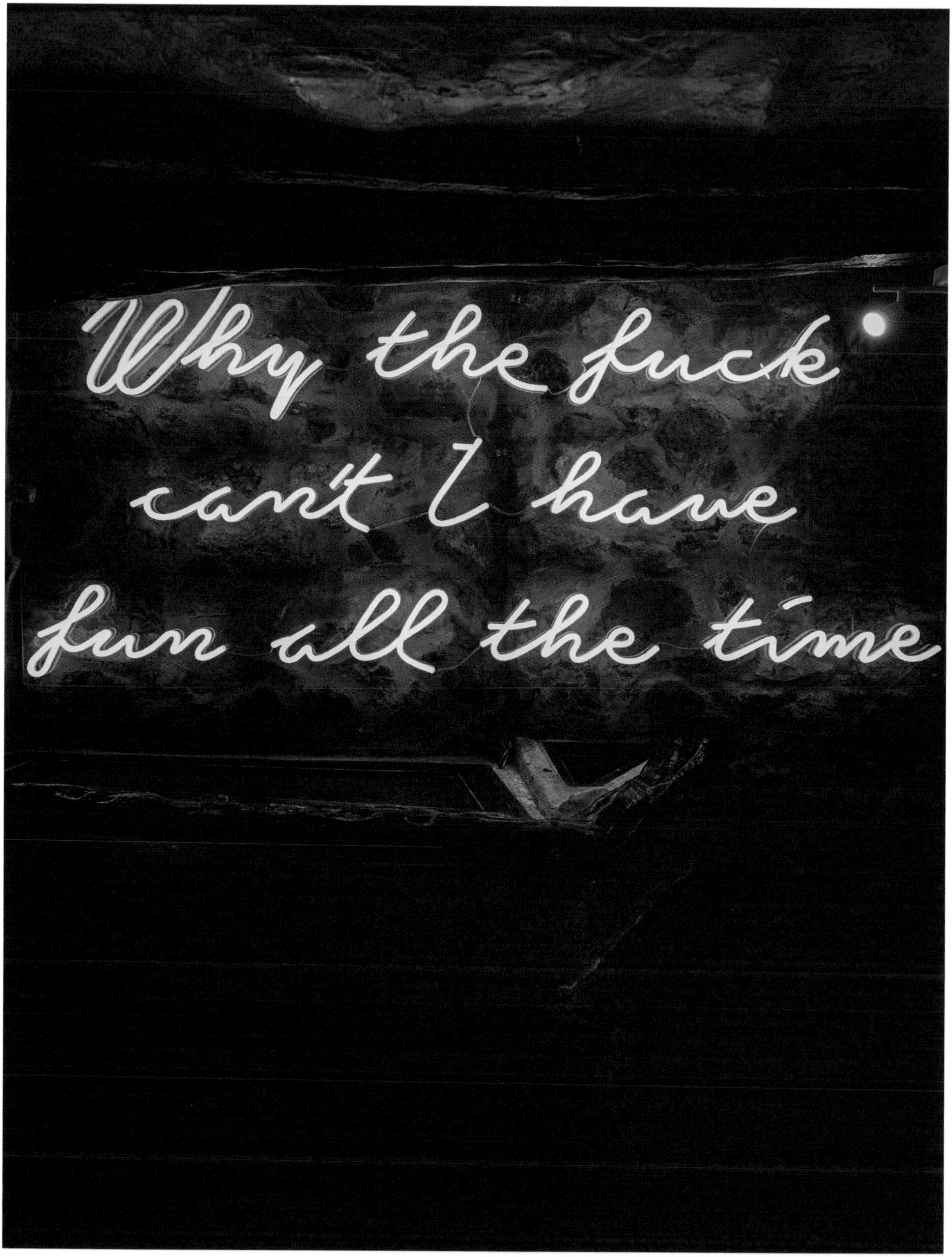
Why the fuck
can't I have
fun all the time

JOSH JOSH JONES

Ingredients

Vanilla vodka
50 ml/1 2/3 fl.oz.
Benedictine
10 ml/1/3 fl.oz.
Pineapple juice
75 ml/2 1/2 fl.oz.
Lemon juice
25 ml/1 fl.oz.
Liquid honey
5 ml/1/6 fl.oz.
Orange bitters
Cubed ice
Garnish: Orange wheel

Serves 1

How to make

Build all of the
ingredients in a
cocktail shaker and add
2 dashes of bitters.
Add cubed ice, shake
well and strain over
fresh cubed ice in a
rocks glass. Garnish
as shown and serve
straightaway.

SILK 'N' FLAVOURS

We incorporated the complex and dominating flavours of Hierbas Ibicencas into this cocktail but the combination of other ingredients hold their own and the juxtaposition of flavours result in this very interesting libation. The smooth mouthfeel and complex depth of flavour are most satisfying.

Ingredients

Gin
30 ml/1 fl.oz.
Cherry liqueur
15 ml/1/2 fl.oz.
Hierbas Ibicencas
10 ml/1/3 fl.oz.
Cointreau
7.5 ml/1/6 fl.oz.
Pineapple juice
80 ml/2 3/4 fl.oz.
Lime juice
15 ml/1/2 fl.oz.
Pomegranate syrup
15 ml/1/2 fl.oz.
Soda water
50 ml/1 2/3 fl.oz.
Angostura bitters
Cherry bitters
Cubed ice
Garnish: Dehydrated
pineapple slice,
Maraschino cherry

Serves 1

How to make

Add all of the ingredients (apart from the soda) to a cocktail shaker and add a dash each of Angostura and cherry bitters. Shake well and strain into an ice-filled sling or highball glass. Add the soda water, garnish as shown and serve straightaway.

HARD PORN

A Pornstar Martini is a combination of vanilla, passion fruit and lime juice flavours, the neutral base liquor is vodka and the fizz comes by way of Cava. By porn standards this would be soft porn. Our hard porn shooter turns the Pornstar into an XXX experience. Using the same ingredients but by adjusting the measurements we aimed to make it hit… hard.

Ingredients

Vanilla vodka
25 ml/1 fl.oz.
Passion fruit purée
5 ml/1/6 fl.oz.
Cava
about 10 ml/1/3 fl.oz.
Lime juice
Sugar syrup

Serves 1

How to make

Scale up the recipe to as many servings as you need and make the base of vanilla vodka and passion fruit purée accordingly. Add a dash each of lime juice and sugar syrup for each serving to the mix. Keep chilled until ready to use. For each serving, pour 30 ml/ 1 fl.oz. of the base mix into a shot glass, top up with chilled Cava and serve straightaway.

COSMOPOLITAN

The Cosmo has its rightful place in the cocktail hall of fame. With a multitude of recipe variations that suited each time and place in which it was tweaked, Cosmopolitans range from very dry to very sweet. Our version is more balanced in terms of sweet, fruit, citrus and alcoholic burn. We choose a flamed orange peel garnish to add a further aromatic goodness.

Ingredients

Vodka
40 ml/1 1/2 fl.oz.
Cointreau
20 ml/3/4 fl.oz.
Cranberry juice
20 ml/3/4 fl.oz.
Lime juice
20 ml/3/4 fl.oz.
Cubed ice
Garnish: Flamed orange peel

Serves 1

How to make

Add all of the ingredients to a Boston shaker glass half-filled with fresh cubed ice. Cover with the shaker and shake well. Strain into a chilled martini glass, garnish with a flamed orange peel and serve straightaway.

Tony's Tale #7

We only had three days to pull Freddie's [Mercury] party together. I told him I could freeze over the pool and get elephants ice skating on it if he really wanted, I just had to have some idea of his budget. Freddie asked me for an idea of what his ideas might cost.
"£50,000" I said.
"£50,000!? That's a great deal of money."
"It's a great deal of party…"
To that he agreed and dismissed me and his manager from the Julio Suite.

Freddie said he had two conditions. One was that it started on Freddie time, which was 7.30pm, and that every guest had to be welcomed with glass of chilled French champagne.

We had people working through the night and lorries trucking stuff in from Barcelona. We had hundreds and hundreds of gold and black balloons festooned all over the courtyard. I had 30 people working for me and we pulled in 70 guys from down on the beach to come and help. I got 10 industrial-sized buckets to put the champagne in and about a ton of ice, which the bar guys then went and used for the cocktails and not for chilling the champagne… I hit the roof when I found that out.

When the guests started to arrive, some of them were already a bit drunk. I used to have a big antique sundial with a giant steel spike right at the entrance and I thought that it looked like it might be a bit dangerous, so I decided to put a champagne cork on the end… One of the guests exclaimed, "Look at that! It looks like a big cock!"

We had about 700 guests, people clamouring to get in, exotic dancers and the infamous firework display. One guy, showing off to a girl, tried to pop a helium balloon with his lighter and the whole wall went up in a sheet of fire, almost melting the overhead cables… but somehow we managed it.
The next day I gave Freddie's manager the very large bill. He pointed to four vodka and tonics on it. "Take them off," he said. "We didn't have any vodkas." Just then, Freddie appeared and said, "I bought those myself for the bar staff." Classic Freddie.

It was a fabulous, fabulous party.

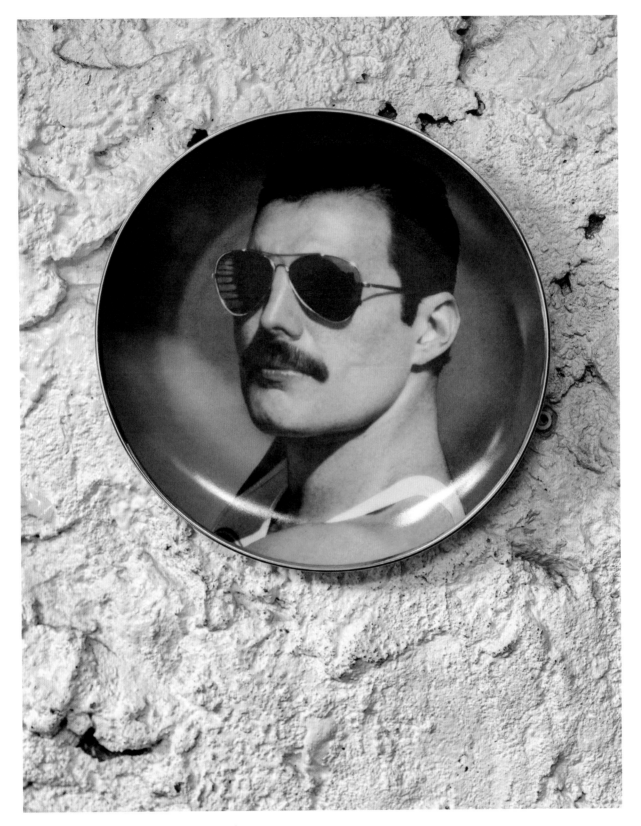

The Morning After

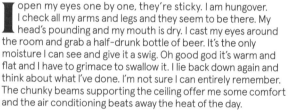

I open my eyes one by one, they're sticky. I am hungover. I check all my arms and legs and they seem to be there. My head's pounding and my mouth is dry. I cast my eyes around the room and grab a half-drunk bottle of beer. It's the only moisture I can see and give it a swig. Oh good god it's warm and flat and I have to grimace to swallow it. I lie back down again and think about what I've done. I'm not sure I can entirely remember. The chunky beams supporting the ceiling offer me some comfort and the air conditioning beats away the heat of the day.

Even blinking hurts.

Things are kind of blurry between doing shots with Lucie and getting to see Harvey play. I definitely remember Harvey – that was a lot of fun. There was a weird bit like at the end of a movie when I could see various characters that make up Pikes Hotel waving and smiling, dancing and drinking. Harvey finished at 4ish, that's for sure. I check my watch - it's half past midday. I vaguely remember going back to one of the big suites, in fact, yes, yes I did. Some of the South London guys had made friends with the people in it and we all went back there for an afterparty. There was a whole lot of people in there. I have a flashback of choreographing a dance routine with Sunny, a travel journalist for a well-known broadsheet and a fashion blogger at one point, that we debuted to the room in front of a wall of mirrors. I'm pretty sure we were pretty good.

My mouth tastes like tequila and my extremely full bladder makes sure I know that it's time to get my shit together and rise and try my best to shine. I realise I've slept in my clothes – trainers and all and figure I might as well wear this outfit to breakfast. Stopping only to brush my teeth and splash a bit of water on my puffy face, I jam on a pair of sunglasses and step out into the daytime. Checking my watch I realise it's 1pm. I head to Room 39 to see

if I can piece together the previous night over some kind of breakfast and friendly, reassuring chit chat.

I try to trot up the steps to the restaurant, failing to find any spring in my step and the first person I spy is Harvey enjoying a cup of tea and full English. I make my way to his table. Starting to comment that he looks pretty spritely I catch myself - of course he does, he's very well practised at this. I settle to telling him his set was incredible. Thanking me like a true gentleman, he tells me he's been up "since the crack of noon" and ushers me to sit down, chuckling at my green gills. As the Pikes cultural attaché I think it's important we should get his opinion on why he likes the place so much. And with a mouthful of toast he tells me.

"Ibiza has been party central for at least 2000 years and I'm one of those people that thinks Ibiza hasn't changed at all, by the way! There has always been a commercial side and an underground side to the place. There are subtle shifts here and there but in general it's still an island in the Mediterranean that people gravitate to, to enjoy themselves and that hasn't changed. The basic idea will remain the same I feel – it's a great place and I always have a great time in Ibiza. I've made great friends and I'd like to think I'm part of the community in some respects. I was an undocumented alien in America for almost a decade and, about five years ago, when I got my Green Card, and returned to the world, I came back to Ibiza and I passed by Pikes. I thought wouldn't it be fantastic to DJ and have a little residency and now I'm basically living that dream.

The island has some of the biggest nightclubs, which I also enjoy doing but what you get with Pikes and Freddie's is almost like a house party. It's very intimate and it has this family vibe and you are amongst the people. There is no other party like it on the island that has the Ibicencan hedonism mixed with the house

party vibe. Even though I might not know half the people there, it's like everyone is a good old friend. Pikes is a cultural oasis, really. It's a very special place, hand-built by Tony Pike so there is a lot of his soul in the walls, and it's got this amazing, long history of grown-up and hedonistic behaviour and things that I enjoy. I've been coming to Ibiza for almost 30 years now and Pikes is somewhere I've visited on a regular basis during that time. I can't say I was there in the glory days of Wham! and Freddie Mercury, but I was there in the late 80s and it's somewhere that's always pulled me towards it.

I've enjoyed several different rooms over the years and I love that every room has a story. Room 26, that's right at the front of the hotel, is quite ornate with the big sunken bath and the one that was the last room that Tony built with the really ornate shower he built for his princess wife. Then, of course, there's the room associated with Julio Iglesias with a secret back entrance and all the music on the walls. Each time when I stay in a different room it's a nice surprise and almost like being in a different hotel as each room has its own character. I love the place."

Harvey couldn't look more at home as he moves around the room chatting to folk like a languid maître d'. Looking around there are a lot of familiar faces looking kind of grey. Some staring into the distance, others with their head in their hands. Gentle Spanish guitar music wafts about the restaurant reassuringly. I figure I should order some avocado on toast - it makes me feel healthy. I take some deep breaths and, to be honest, focus on settling my sudden queasiness. A waiter brushes past me carrying what might be my salvation on a tray to Rebecca Tay, the travel journalist from last night's after party. Of course! I always forget this until I see someone drinking one. I need a Bloody Mary, or here a

Sunday Roast - the Pikes take on the classic drink. If anything will ward off the looming hangover, that should help. I make my way over to Rebecca and find out her story. Originally from Canada she writes for big boy papers like the *Telegraph* and *Wall Street Journal* but her involvement with Pikes is more personal. "I'm part of the extended Pikes family, which basically means I used to go out with someone who is part of the direct Manumission/ Ibiza Rocks/Pikes family. I actually remember when Dawn and Andy took Pikes on - it was a huge undertaking but also so exciting, and seeing it take shape together was pretty special. I was lucky enough to go on a buying trip in the UK with Dawn, where we acquired some of the wacky, weird and wonderful things you can see around the hotel – the sheep sign in the tennis court, the hand-shaped chairs on the front lawn, the taxidermied ostrich foot and various other preserved creatures. Watching Dawn purchase those items as one-offs was a bit nerve-racking as it could have all gone so wrong. But that's exactly what I love about Pikes – how it's more than a bit peculiar but also so quirky and fun. There's always something new to look at - which is especially fun when you've had a few drinks or are re-emerging after a couple of hours spent in Sunny's boudoir..."

I catch the waiter's attention on his way back to the bar and whisper my order. He pats me gently on the shoulder and tells me everything will be OK, it's definitely not the first one he's had to make today.

Guests, staff, DJs, princes, singers, writers – they all make up the diverse cast of the hotel and all play their part in keeping it a very special place. If, as Nostradamus predicted in the 15th century, Ibiza is the only place to survive the end of the world, then you know where to find us all. We'll be sitting at the bar in Pikes.

RISING SUN

Ingredients

Bourbon
50 ml/1 2/3 fl.oz.
Maple syrup
15 ml/1/2 fl.oz.
Cream
20 ml/3/4 fl.oz.
1 whole fresh egg
Cubed ice
Garnish: Ground
cinnamon or nutmeg,
as preferred

Serves 1

How to make

First dry shake the egg
in a cocktail shaker
(i.e. without ice).
Add all of the other
ingredients and cubed
ice, shake and strain
into a small, long-
stemmed wine glass.
Dust with ground
cinnamon or nutmeg
and serve straightaway.

CARAJILLO & CAFÉ BOMBON

Ingredients	How to make
Carajillo: Brandy (or other liquor of your choice, try whisky or anisette) Espresso shot Sugar to taste Milk foam (optional)	To make the Carajillo, add a shot of warmed brandy (and sugar to taste) to a small coffee glass. Add a shot of hot, freshly made espresso coffee. Top with milk foam (if desired) and serve.
Café Bombon: Condensed milk to taste Espresso shot Each recipe serves 1	To make the Café Bombon, add the preferred amount of condensed milk to a small coffee glass. Add a shot of hot, freshly made espresso coffee and serve.

SLIPPERY WHEN WET

Ingredients

Tequila
60 ml/2 fl.oz.
Passion fruit purée
25 ml/1 fl.oz.
Liquid honey
40 ml/1 1/2 fl.oz.
Thumbnail-size skinned
aloe vera piece
1/4 fresh peach
(see #note)
Crushed ice
Garnish: Peach slice,
passion fruit slice,
mint sprig

Serves 1

How to make

Add all of the
ingredients to a
blender with 3/4 scoop
of crushed ice. Blend
to create a frozen
slush. Pour into
a large coupe glass,
garnish as shown and
serve straightaway.

#note: Using fresh
peach slices that have
been frozen before use
will help to create the
desired consistency.

TIC 'N' TOC

Around Pikes you can't but help notice our obsession with time. We insist that you always make time to try one of our cocktails. Tic 'n' Toc is a take on a classic Mojito but opts for lemon rather than lime, and vodka and elderflower liqueur in place of the rum. This cocktail is delicately floral with minty freshness and a soft citrus kick.

Ingredients

Vodka
30 ml/1 fl.oz.
Elderflower liqueur
25 ml/1 fl.oz.
Gomme syrup
10 ml/1/3 fl.oz.
10 fresh mint leaves
1/3 of a Lemon
Soda water to top up
Crushed ice
Garnish: Lemon slices, mint sprig

Serves 1

How to make

Muddle the lemon in a highball glass. Add the mint leaves and gently bruise. Add the gomme syrup, vodka and elderflower liqueur then add crushed ice to half-fill the glass. Stir with a barspoon, top up with soda water and stir again. Fill to the top with more crushed ice, garnish as shown and serve straightaway.

BABY JANE

Ingredients

Vanilla vodka
25 ml/1 fl.oz.
Crème de cacao blanc
15 ml/1/2 fl.oz.
Banana purée
5 ml/1/6 fl.oz.
Orange juice
50 ml/1 2/3 fl.oz.
1 Small red chilli
Cubed ice
Garnish: Sugar syrup,
popping candy to rim
the glass

Serves 1

How to make

Moisten the rim of
a chilled martini glass
with sugar syrup. Put
the crushed popping
candy on a plate and
dip the glass into it
to rim it. Muddle the
chilli in a cocktail
shaker and then add the
other ingredients. Add
cubed ice, shake and
double strain into the
chilled cocktail glass.
Serve straightaway.

BLOODY MARY

Ingredients

Vodka
50 ml/1 2/3 fl.oz.
Tomato juice
90 ml/3 fl.oz.
Lemon juice
15 ml/1/2 fl.oz.
Worcestershire sauce
Tabasco sauce
Celery salt
Black pepper
1/4 tsp finely grated
fresh horseradish
Cubed ice
Garnish: Celery stalk,
lemon slice, cherry
tomato

Serves 1

How to make

Combine the vodka and
juices in a Boston
shaker glass over cubed
ice. Add 4 dashes of
Worcestershire sauce
and 2 dashes of Tabasco
sauce plus a pinch
each of celery salt
and pepper. Pour from
glass to shaker and
back again a few times.
Leave in the shaker.
Add fresh cubed ice
to a highball glass
and pour the drink in.
Garnish as shown and
serve straightaway.

COMEBACK KID

The Comeback Kid is symbolic at Pikes. At some stage, almost everyone finds themselves trying to make a comeback from the excesses. This shot is 100% natural and boasts medicinal properties. Although not designed to be enjoyed orally, the anti inflammatory properties and vitamin bomb support the body against the sins of excess. We recommend you start the day with one… Or two.

Ingredients

Freshly squeezed juice of 2 small oranges
Freshly squeezed juice of 2 small lemons
35 g/1/4 Cup peeled, chopped fresh turmeric
35 g/1/4 Cup peeled, chopped fresh ginger
1/8 tsp Ground black pepper
1/4 tsp Extra virgin olive oil
Handful of goji berries
CBD oil (optional)

Serves 4

How to make

Add all of the ingredients except the CBD oil to a blender and blend until smooth. Strain into a small jug/pitcher and then pour into 4 small glasses (shot or liqueur will do). Add a few drops of CBD oil to each one (optional) and serve straightaway.

Tony's Tale #8

Frank Zappa came here and I didn't know who he was – he looked like he couldn't buy a coffee; he looked like a hobo. A group of people took him out for lunch and I tagged along. Afterwards, Frank stood up and said as he'd just flown in from New York he wanted to go back to the hotel before the evening so I offered to give him a lift back.

We were driving along and he said I didn't know who he was. "Course I do, you're Frank Zappa," I said. "Who's Frank Zappa?" "You're Frank Zappa." "Who's Frank Zappa?" "I just fucking told you, you're Frank Zappa." It could have gone on forever. He thought it was refreshing to meet someone who wasn't on the take from him. We were sitting in the bar and he asked me whether the fact he'd just spent $3m impressed me. As I was just working on this place it really didn't. Frank said he had a proposition for me and ran to Room 1 and came back with a leather briefcase. He pulled out this Russian document and all I could understand were the numbers $2.7m, which was for a property he'd just bought not far from the Kremlin. He said with the other $300k he'd bought a vodka factory and thought we should make a Pikes Peach Vodka; he had people making the brews and we could make it world-famous. Then he asked me if we could open up Pikes boutique-style hotels around the world – if he found a property he'd fly me over to set it up and I'd make 15% off the top.

A while later Frank rang me up saying he'd found the perfect place for the first Pikes Hotel franchise. It was Havana, Cuba – Ernest Hemingway's old house. He said he'd told Fidel that I was a nice man and "not to worry about Gorbachev" as he was on side too. I told him I'd be straight over; he really wanted to get on with it. Then he only fucking died on me...

Art direction and Design:
Gerard Saint & Phil Armson at Big Active.
Photography: Kim Lightbody.
Text: Josh Jones.
Recipes: Steve Hughes.
Commissioning Editor: Pete Jorgensen.
Editorial Director: Julia Charles.
Production Manager: Gordana Simakovic.
Publisher: Cindy Richards.

First published in 2020 by
Ryland Peters & Small
20-21 Jockey's Fields
London WC1R 4BW
and 341 E 116th St
New York NY 10029.

www.rylandpeters.com

10 9 8 7 6 5 4 3 2 1

ISBN: 978-1-78879-212-7

A CIP record for this book is available from the British Library.
US Library of Congress CIP data has been applied for.

Printed in China